FULL CIRCLE

Race, Law & Justice

Third World Press Foundation
Publishers since 1967
Chicago

Full Circle
Race, Law & Justice
© 2018 James D. Montgomery, Sr.

First Edition
Printed in the United States of America
22 21 20 19 18   6 5 4 3 2 1

Library of Congress Control Number: 2017954338
ISBN: 978-0-88378-400-6 | Paperback

Editor: Paulette Nunlee
Cover design and interior layout by
Sean Hicks of Gargoyle Creative Services & Design

Dedication

To my late father, James Livingston Montgomery, who assured me when I was a teenager that "I was as good as anybody" as well as my beloved wife Pauline Montgomery and children Linda, James, Jr., Michelle, Lisa, Jewel and Jilian whose generosity, support, and stability made my journey possible and meaningful.

FULL CIRCLE

Race, Law & Justice

Inside My Life
Atty. James D. Montgomery, Sr.

**Walter M. Perkins
& Michelle Thompson**

TABLE OF CONTENTS

James D. Montgomery Jr.
Concert Band
Trigonometry Club
Drama Club
Student Council
Lawyer

A Trial Lawyer Is...

"In many ways, a trial lawyer is like an actor on stage. His lines are not always scripted, and that makes his job harder. He has to react, to be quick on his feet and with his tongue, to know when to attack and when to shut up, when to lead and when to follow, when to flash anger and when to be cool. Through it all, he's got to convince and persuade because nothing matters but the jury's final vote."

John Grisham
"Rogue Lawyer"

Over the past six decades, **Atty. James D. Montgomery, Sr.** has transformed a blank canvas into a colorful legal landscape of successful civil and criminal cases. Some of these cases will be discussed, analyzed, and written about for years to come.

Overwhelmingly, those who know Montgomery professionally respect him immensely. This is due—in large part—to his relentless dedication to serving his clients and desire to master the practice of law. As a result, his legal colleagues are the best barometers for measuring the place he holds in Chicago's turbulent legal history and offering critical insight into the characteristics that have served him well in such a climate.

WORDS OF HIGH PRAISE FOR ATTY. MONTGOMERY

Judge Walter Williams, Retired

"Excellent and very professional. Thorough. Knows applicable law, the facts, strengths, and weaknesses of his cases. Thoroughly prepares his witnesses to testify on direct and cross-examination."

Atty. Walter Jones, Jr.

"Dynamic and energetic. The moment he speaks people take notice. His opening statements and cross-examination techniques make Jim better than anyone else."

Atty. Lewis Myers, Jr.

"Excellent trial lawyer. He is a person of respect and integrity. Most importantly, he is sincerely dedicated to fighting for the rights of African Americans across the country."

Atty. Thomas Marszewski

"Thoughtful, thorough, loves being a lawyer. Fierce competitor, well prepared, great taskmaster. Mesmerizes juries, especially in closing arguments. Brings a rare theatrical quality to the courtroom. Well-respected statesman."

Atty. Elvin E. Charity

"I was a young assistant corporation counsel, working under Atty. Montgomery in the Harold Washington administration. Following another lawyer's poorly prepared and presented response, Jim told the lawyer, 'You don't know

what the fuck you're talking about.' I learned not to go into a meeting unprepared."

Judge Daniel Locallo

"He has a very unique voice. If he calls you, it's almost as if God is talking. He is meticulous, has a good presence, and fights hard for his clients. He knows his cases, the strengths and weaknesses. He is professional in dealings with attorneys and judges."

A biography is a documented history of one's life, including the good, the bad, the highs, and the lows.

The best ones recognize that even the most heroic subjects often possess the most tragic flaws.

The unbiased eye of an authentic biography wields a scalpel, painfully stripping away the scar tissue of one's life.

It takes courage to authorize this kind of scrutiny, the kind of courage that is often lacking in many potential subjects.

A successful biography offers a person insights they might have overlooked or buried in the deepest recesses of their minds.

A successful biography might spur a subject to become a better person.

Or, it might awaken the vanity that lurks in the psyche of even the best of us.

At the very least, a well-sourced biography sorts through the urban legends and outright lies that shadow the lives of many public figures.

In a candid, sweeping interview with Co-Author Walter M. Perkins, Atty. James D. Montgomery, Sr., offers his uncensored views on racism and the U.S. Justice System.

WP: By your senior year at Wendell Phillips High School, you had decided to become a lawyer so you could affect social change. At some point, you realized that the law itself was racist and oppressive, not supportive of African Americans as you had originally believed.

JDM: Like every young, vulnerable, and gullible student who has studied civics and history, I was told about the **American Dream** and I bought it. I assumed it was true and that was how life would be if you worked hard and were a law-abiding member of society. I believed you could go as far as your abilities would take you.

WP: What happened?

JDM: When I began practicing law in Chicago, I looked at the political situation. That's when I saw that the deck was stacked against black people politically, and in the judicial system.

WP: Any specific recollections?

JDM: Early on, when I first appeared before a white judge, he disrespected my boss, and nothing was done. Later, when I began to handle small cases on my own, I experienced judges who berated my clients while I was sitting there representing them. I learned that it was a racist system from the first day I became a lawyer.

WP: You built your reputation by often representing notorious clients who were in difficult legal situations, as both a criminal defense attorney and civil attorney in high-profile police shooting cases. Can you share some of your thinking and approach in civil cases?

JDM: My practice—whenever there was a police killing, especially where there was questionable police conduct—was to call a press conference in my office. In front of the media and television cameras, I would blast away at the police. That was both business promotion and an attempt to influence public opinion. I wanted people to understand that the police were using excessive force.

WP: No concern about tainting the jury pool?

JDM: I didn't care if I did.

WP: Are you making a political statement when you take these kinds of cases?

JDM: Every time. In the press conference, I say, "The problem here is that police officers are condoned in their shooting of black people. It continues because they are not punished, fired, or suspended. They don't make the police pay a dime when the city is ordered to pay out millions of dollars."

WP: Are there more black victims of police shootings today, or does the media just make it seem that way?

JDM: No question about it. You don't read anything in the paper about any white people being killed by the police. It's rare that you even see a case where police brutalize a white person.

That speaks volumes because the police presence is mostly in the black community. Those patrolling the black community are mostly white officers who don't live in the community and don't respect black people. They also fear black people. They are likely to be as scared of law-abiding citizens as they are of real criminals.

WP: What role do drugs play?

JDM: If drugs were not proliferating in our community, then I don't think the police would be as scared. I also don't think there would be the number of killings we have today with black-on-black crime and shootings by the police.

WP: What now?

JDM: The only real solution is the swift punishment of those police officers found to have violated a person's rights or who have taken a person's life without justification. No police officer should remain on the job once a twelve-person jury has found that he or she wrongfully killed someone. This type of police officer has no business on the police force.

WP: What about the rampant gun violence in Chicago?

JDM: Two things: One, guns are not the problem. It's the people who acquire and use guns. In our community, guns go hand in hand with drugs, drug sales and competition for drug sales. Guns go hand in hand with gangs. Secondly, drugs and gangs are the stuff from which black-on-black crime is created and sustained.

WP: Any suggestions on solving those issues?

JDM: I believe that you've got to legalize drugs—the same thing that was done with Prohibition and alcohol. You've got to tax the products and remove the profit motive. That eliminates the motive for killing people. What are the details needed? I don't know. You need smarter people than me for that.

WP: It worked with alcohol. Is there a reason this hasn't been done?

JDM: Yes. The infrastructure in the United States that "fights" the war on drugs is so pervasive and costly. If drugs were legalized it would cause a recession and all of these people and agencies would be thrown out of work. They're failing. They're failing on purpose. If this country wanted to stop drugs from crossing the borders, we're smart enough to do it. We just don't choose to do so.

WP: Let's shift a little. Is the deck stacked in favor of the prosecution in criminal cases? If so, how?

JDM: Yes, the prosecution has the money, resources, and staff to thoroughly prepare their cases. They also benefit from a system that is stacked against the accused in a very biased way. But it's stacked against the accused whether they are black or white. Why? The answer is because— in one manner or another—the establishment selects the judges.

WP: How so?

JDM: It's less so today than it was in earlier years. But still, you've largely got to be an acceptable type of candidate. People understand that to be acceptable, you must be mainstream. To be mainstream, you must be tough on crime.

Many judges start off being tough on crime before they've decided whether the defendant is a criminal. So, sometimes the deck is stacked against you from the judge's perspective. Sometimes, it's just an imbalance of resources.

WP: So, the defense is, shall we say, defenseless?

JDM: Most people who commit crimes don't have any real money. Take even drug dealers. By the time they get to a serious case, they don't have any money. Cash is "easy come, easy go." And when they do hire a lawyer, they have to hire him with short money. And, they usually get short shrift on the lawyer's services.

WP: I've heard more than one defense attorney say, "You can indict a ham sandwich." This can't be true, is it?

JDM: Oh, yes. There's no question about that because the grand jury is the prosecution's handmaiden. If the prosecution can go in and articulate something and ask for an indictment, they usually get it.

WP: And the defense has virtually no rights in front of a grand jury?

JDM: The defense has no lawyer, with one exception. A defendant who is the subject of a grand jury investigation—if being called as a witness—has the right to his lawyer in private before he answers a question. Otherwise, witnesses are in there with only the prosecution and the grand jurors.

WP: Does your experience as a former prosecutor give you an advantage on the defense side? If so, how?

JDM: Yes, the prosecution has the burden of establishing guilt. When you've had that experience of knowing what you have to prove and how you have to sell it, then it helps you on the defense side because you know exactly what you have to overcome.

WP: So, it's always an advantage?

JDM: Well, I remember Eugene Pincham told me one time when we were co-counsels, "Damn it! Jim, you think like a goddamn prosecutor." So, sometimes—you know—it might be a burden (laughing).

22

WP: Is it your view that at the start of a typical case, most judges favor the prosecution?

JDM: That may have been the case in the past. Today, there are more independent judges because they don't have to present themselves before the political parties, the powers that be. Judges are more independent than in years past because of the sub-districts, which means more judges are elected.

WP: Any examples?

JDM: The late Judge Leo Holt, both a former law partner and client. He was elected and became as independent as you could imagine any judge to be. Certainly, no one could ever say that any defendant who came before him felt that they were disadvantaged or that the prosecution had an advantage. He is a good example, but it's not true across the board.

WP: What kind of research do you do on judges once they are assigned to your case?

JDM: In the old days, when I was in the courthouse every day, lawyers would talk to each other about the judges. You pretty much got the lowdown from fellow lawyers. Today, there are a bunch of judges up there of whom you've never heard. Again, you reach out to colleagues and ask about judges. You go to the Sullivan's Law Directory that has background information on judges. That's about it.

WP: If you could select any judge in history to hear a case, who would it be and why?

JDM: Judge Blanche Manning, a former federal court judge. Before that, she was a state appellate court judge and a state trial judge. You could count on receiving a complete, fair hearing. She wouldn't give you anything. But, she wouldn't take away anything from you. She would allow you to try your case without interference. She would not show—in any way—what her opinion was about the case.

WP: Let's talk about juries. Have you used jury consultants?

JDM: One time on the Black Panther case. It's helpful because you need all of the information you can get. But, ultimately, you must make a judgment by looking at people, talking to them, and getting a feel from their body language and how they respond to you.

WP: Have you ever lost a case because you misread a jury?

JDM: I have lost cases where jurors were wrong for my case. You have to sell a jury. Some jurors you are never going to be able to get rid of unless you can prove bias. That's difficult because people usually want to be selected. So, they give you the answer that they think you're looking for. Judges are impatient with jury selection nowadays. In federal court, some judges will do most of the questioning themselves.

WP: I have heard it said that it's not necessarily in the best interests for an African American client to have an all African American jury. What is your feeling?

JDM: Black folks are very complex. Some are regular victims of crime, making them wary of anyone who is accused. It depends on the jurisdiction. Lawyers in Washington, D.C. tell me that they hate black juries. They don't want them because all-black juries are sometimes hard on their people.

WP: Finally, what kind of juror do you avoid at all costs?

JDM: Someone whom you believe is biased against either your client or your theory of the case.

WP: **Thank you Atty. Montgomery.**

Book titles are important, serving as a first encounter between the subject, author, and reader. Sometimes, titles promise more than they deliver. Occasionally, they deliver more than they promise.

The authors and researchers of *Full Circle* have been gathering primary and secondary research since **May, 2015**. Because the book's subject, **Atty. James D. Montgomery, Sr.**, has been a public figure for more than fifty years, the public record yields a great deal. Multiple in-depth interviews with Atty. Montgomery have revealed a person with deep and honest reflections about his life, his impact on society, and how his family, peers, and history will recall him and his contributions.

His contributions have been many and varied, having impacted **law, civil rights, politics, civic affairs, philanthropy**, and **higher education**.

As we explored the inner sanctum of Montgomery's life, it seemed the more information we unearthed about past events, the more things seemed to be the same today. Or, there is so little difference, one would hardly notice.

Unless you pay close attention to evolving historical events, you might think police brutality against blacks, school segregation, and unfair housing practices are new developments in American culture.

Let's take the issue of police brutality in Chicago.

> *"The Mayor doesn't understand what happens to black*
> *men on the streets of Chicago, and probably never will."*

U.S. Congressman, Ralph Harold Metcalfe

Of course, the mayor whom **Congressman Metcalfe** referenced was not **Rahm Emanuel**, but the powerful **Chicago Mayor Richard J. Daley**. Congressman Metcalfe made the statement in **1972** after he became enraged about Daley's inattention to several events, including the infamous Chicago police raid on **Black Panther Fred Hampton's apartment**. This tragic event occurred on **December 4, 1969** and resulted in Chicago police **murdering Illinois Black Panther leader, Fred Hampton**, as well as **Mark Clark**, a panther from **Peoria, Illinois**.

Media sources and others present in the apartment reported that Hampton and Clark were sleeping at the time of the raid, which occurred at approximately 4:45 a.m. **Montgomery** later represented **Fred Hampton's family,** winning a $1.8 million settlement in a civil lawsuit.

Also during the early seventies, there had been several other confrontations between some Chicago Police Department officers and black citizens, including the highly publicized harassment of two black dentists, which led to Congressman Metcalfe's break with Daley and the Democratic Machine.

The congressman's actions shook the white political establishment to its core, considering that Metcalfe had been both a close friend and political ally of Mayor Daley.

l-r: Jesse Owens and Ralph Metcalfe, 1936

l-r: Jesse Owens and Ralph Metcalfe, 1936 Olympics

The **2016** movie *Race* chronicled the **1936 Olympics** in **Berlin**, focusing on **Jesse Owens, winner of four gold medals**. The movie ignored **Ralph Metcalfe** who, like Jesse Owens, captured **four Olympic medals: one gold, two silver, and one bronze**. And though history has mostly downplayed Metcalfe's contribution, there is a lasting legacy in downtown Chicago, the **Ralph H. Metcalfe Federal Building**.

In a report released after Congressman Metcalfe convened a congressional hearing investigating complaints of police brutality by the Chicago Police Department, he denounced the department as *"rotten to the core."*

*Source – Chicago Tribune (U.S. House of Representatives: History, Art & Archives)

Fast-forward to February 15, 2016, when Chicago Sun-Times columnist Laura Washington wrote:

"Just a presidential helicopter ride away from his adopted city, the place he calls home, black Chicagoans are reeling from a triple terror: a viciously high murder rate, decades-long history of police abuse and misconduct, and pernicious unemployment and poverty."

Washington was offering an epilogue to **President Barack Obama's** sixty-minute unity speech to the Illinois General Assembly, which the president delivered just five days earlier on **February 10th**. The president began his political career as an Illinois state senator, before being elected to the U.S. Senate, on the way to becoming the **first African American President of the United States**.

He returned to **Springfield, Illinois**, site of the start of his swift rise to the top, urging former colleagues to seek common ground, hoping they would toss aside political differences and finally pass a balanced state budget.

During most of **2016**, the **Illinois General Assembly** was locked in a months-long budget impasse, with **first-term Republican Governor Bruce Rauner**. The year began with the state of Illinois on the edge of insolvency, the public education system threatening to shut down, and statewide programs serving the poor and disabled closing.

Montgomery, reflecting on his long history of fighting the system says:

> *Some of the reasons we are in this condition include economic deprivation, poverty, and lack of opportunity. Another thing is the prevalence of drugs in our community.*
>
> *I have spent a good deal of the last thirty years fighting the police department and police tactics.*

After all of that effort and time, he sometimes wonders if it has made a difference:

> *You go to court, establish that these officers have wrongfully killed somebody and they're still working. The police officers don't pay a dime. There are no consequences. So, they continue as if it's a policy and okay.*
>
> *Police brutality was rampant in the sixties and seventies, and it was no different from what it is today in terms of there being an outright disrespect for black people by the police department and complete suppression of any misconduct or killings that the police did to black people.*
>
> *So, we are living in that same climate today; it has not changed at all. The bottom line is that it is wonderful to see that there is some movement directly focused on self-defense against police injustice. I am encouraged by the fact that we have some degree of restlessness among concerned citizens.*
>
> *How well we do? I don't know; I hope that it does not fizzle because it would be wonderful if this dynamic energy could blossom into a continuous movement that would end up making some difference.*
>
> *I think that just like in the seventies, it's not too much different today. If we were not so impoverished today, people could focus on things that are more important to them rather than going out to fight a system that they think is intractable.*
>
> *I just have a notion that until we figure out a way to free ourselves economically and politically, it ain't gon' happen.*

So, the unfortunate fact is that today's headlines mirror those of twenty, thirty, even forty years ago. Where are we as a community of African Americans headed in Chicago and nationwide?

Some might argue that regarding the issues of quality of life, economics, self-love, race relations and police brutality, we've come *Full Circle*, right back where we were decades ago.

> *"Most black folks who are surviving in this economy live by compromise. Can't afford to be assertive about anything. Have to be proper Negroes to succeed."*

Atty. James D. Montgomery, Sr.
July 25, 2015

Chapter 01
EARLY INFLUENCE

"You do what you think is right and let the law catch up."

Thurgood Marshall

A young, black man coming of age in the late 1940s and early 1950s had to keep his ear close to the ground to find a role model if he wanted to become a lawyer.

Thanks, or no thanks, to the image of the bumbling, shyster "black lawyer," **Algonquin J. Calhoun**. In the 1950s, when images of black attorneys were unfavorable and demeaning, this caricature was widely spread by the **white creators** of "**Amos 'n' Andy**."

Fortunately, during law school, and throughout James D. Montgomery's legal career, his role model, Thurgood Marshall, wielded considerable influence over him—and his career.

Thurgood Marshall

THURGOOD MARSHALL REWOUND

Originally named **Thoroughgood**, Marshall later shortened the name by changing the spelling. Born in **Baltimore, Maryland** in **1908**, he graduated **magna cum laude** from **Howard University Law School** in **1933**, one year after **Montgomery** was born in **Louise, Mississippi**.

Immediately after graduation, Thurgood Marshall began practicing in Baltimore. Soon after, in 1934, he began his longtime affiliation with the **NAACP** by representing them in a law school discrimination suit, *Murray v. Pearson*.

In this case, the **University of Maryland Law School** denied a black **Amherst College graduate** admission. Atty. Marshall sued the school on the theory that *Plessy v. Ferguson's separate but equal clause*, then still in force, was violated because Maryland did not provide *"a comparable educational opportunity at a state-run black institution."* He won the case on appeal to the **Maryland Court of Appeals**. In **1936**, Marshall joined the NAACP staff.

Much like Justice Marshall, Montgomery has also spent considerable time using the law to seek justice, including challenging Chicago's segregated public school system in the 1960s and 1970s. Montgomery explains:

"My legal career has been a career of fighting the system. It has been a career of working pro bono for a lot of people who were trying to do some good for our community."

"During the sixties and seventies, I engaged in civil litigation against the Chicago Board of Education...when we started having sit-downs in the street, and so forth. Whenever there were mass arrests, I was one of the lawyers who volunteered my services."

In **1963** and **1964**, **Chicago Public Schools** was hit with two massive student boycotts, resulting from the city's continued maintenance of a segregated and racist public school system. According to the **Chicago Grassroots Curriculum Taskforce**, in a **2013 report** commemorating the boycotts, groups representing the black, Hispanic, and even white communities believed that black students were being discriminated against in five major ways:

1. **Funding inequities**

2. **Less qualified and experienced teachers**

3. **Overcrowding**

4. **Focus on European and Anglo-American based curriculum**

5. **Willis Wagons (trailers used as classrooms for black students)**

On **October 22, 1963**, between **200,000** and **225,000** students (actual numbers vary) boycotted the schools. The boycott was followed by another walkout on **February 25, 1964**, where another **172,350** students found other things to do rather than continue participating in a segregated school system. The **Chicago Grassroots Curriculum Taskforce** reported this information.

Following are key historical events leading up to the student boycotts:

Noted author, **Dempsey Travis**, also an activist and real estate developer who specialized in books documenting Chicago history, wrote in *An Autobiography of Black Politics*:

"In 1960, picketers marched around the Chicago Board of Education to protest the "double shift" schools that were implemented in black communities even though 50,000 seats were open in one

l-r, Dempsey Travis with James D. Montgomery, Sr. in the early 1980s

32

*hundred and seventy schools where white students attended, according to a report by Chicago's chapter of **Committee of Racial Equality (CORE)**."*

Continuing, Travis writes that in 1961:

*"**James Montgomery**, a black lawyer and political activist at the time, put the fear of God into then superintendent, **Benjamin C. Willis**, in the federal courts when he challenged de-facto segregation in the Chicago schools, seeking an injunction to end it."*

"Montgomery ultimately negotiated the school case and got some relief. The lawsuit represented an adventure in the "art of the possible" because Superintendent Willis never regained his balance of power and finally resigned in 1966."

Authors' Note: Willis offered his resignation on October 4, 1963, following an announcement at a press conference. However, the Chicago Board of Education refused to accept his resignation, later working out a compromise.

So, it is clear that Thurgood Marshall was among a handful of black, legal activists in the middle of the twentieth century who paved the way for black lawyers like **R. Eugene Pincham, Kermit Coleman, Johnny Cochran, Lewis Myers, Jr.** and, yes, James D. Montgomery, Sr.

Supreme Court Justice
Thurgood Marshall

HIGHLIGHTS – JUSTICE THURGOOD MARSHALL

- **1961 – Appointed to U.S. Court of Appeals (Second Circuit) – President Kennedy**

- **1965 – First African American U.S. Solicitor General – President Johnson**

- **1967 – First African American Supreme Court Justice – President Johnson**

- **Won twenty-nine of thirty-two cases argued before the Supreme Court**

- **Won fourteen of nineteen cases while U.S. Solicitor General**

Justice Marshall served on the **Supreme Court from October, 1967** until **October, 1991**, when he stepped down due to health issues. He passed on January 24, 1993. He spent his twenty-four years on the court, often joined by **Justice William Brennan**, advocating Constitutional protection of **individual rights**, especially the rights of **criminal suspects** against the government.

As the NAACP's chief counsel, Thurgood Marshall argued the landmark case, ***Brown v. the Board of Education of Topeka, 347 U.S. 483, (1954)**, before the Supreme Court. It is often referred to as "Brown I."* In **Brown I**, the Supreme

Court struck down the *separate but equal requirement of Plessy v. Ferguson*, ruling that state laws establishing separate public schools for black and white students are unconstitutional. The ruling meant that, going forward, separate facilities were inherently unequal.

Ruby Bridges, a beneficiary of Brown decision, with her U.S. Marshalls escorts

Brown II handed down in **1955** fleshed out how to apply the court's requirement that desegregation should proceed with *"all deliberate speed."* Ultimately, the decision in Brown served as the foundation for Montgomery to fight against segregation in Chicago Public Schools.

The following quote from **Justice Thurgood Marshall** sums up his **legacy**, and continued importance to the struggles and aspirations of **African Americans** and society in general.

> *We must dissent from the indifference. We must dissent from the apathy. We must dissent from the fear, the hatred and the mistrust. We must dissent from a nation that has buried its head in the sand, waiting in vain for the needs of its poor, its elderly and its sick to disappear and just blow away. We must dissent from a government that has left its young without jobs, education or hope. We must dissent from the poverty of vision and the absence of moral leadership. We must dissent because America can do better, because America has no choice but to do better.*

Sound familiar? Dissent indeed.

Authors' Note: Most cases argued and won before the Supreme Court occurred when Thurgood Marshall headed the NAACP Legal Defense Fund.

Chapter 02

IN THE BEGINNING
— LOUISE, MISSISSIPPI

"If anyone should ever write my life story,
for whatever reason there might be…"

Gladys Knight – Singer

There are many reasons to write the life story of **noted activist and civil rights attorney, James D. Montgomery, Sr.**

Here are just a few:

- **Legendary litigator – criminal defense and personal injury**
- **Top tier civil rights attorney**
- **Mayor Harold Washington's Corporation Counsel**
- **Principal and licensee – Johnny Cochran's national law firm**
- **Attorney for Fred Hampton family – the civil trial**
- **University of Illinois Board Trustee**
- **Philanthropist**

Nevertheless, it all began on **February 17, 1932** in **Louise, Mississippi**, where the current population is **one hundred and ninety-nine** according to the **2010 U.S. Census**: broken down, that's eighty-five blacks, one hundred and thirteen whites, and one other. Even with those figures, Louise is a metropolis compared to the nearby town of **Midnight, Mississippi**, with a population of one hundred and fifty-five as recorded in the 2010 Census, with one hundred and thirty-four blacks, twenty whites, and one other.

Louise, Mississippi is not a vacation destination and not coveted by real estate developers. To date, it is not known to be a source of oil, gold, precious metals, or any other valuable resource.

Readers are no doubt more familiar with **Jackson**, the state capital; **Tunica** the casino mecca; **Biloxi** and **Greenville**, site of the annual **Mississippi Delta Blues and Heritage Festival**. There is probably no reason to visit Louise, Mississippi unless you are in search of the birthplace of James D. Montgomery, Sr.

The year **1932** was important not just for the Montgomery family. Events happening in the United States and globally were setting the tone for the twentieth century and the world we live in today.

In 1932:

- The Great Depression spreads worldwide
- Franklin Delano Roosevelt elected to the first of four presidential terms
- Andrew Young, associate of Dr. King, U.N. Ambassador, and U.S. Congressman from Georgia, is born
- Al Capone convicted of tax evasion
- Publication of first black daily newspaper, Atlanta Daily World
- Charles Lindbergh's son kidnapped
- NAACP's Springarn Medal awarded to Robert R. Moton, President of Tuskegee Institute

On the economic front:

- U.S. unemployment rate – 24%
- Average new home - $6,500
- Average annual wage - $1,650
- Gallon of gas - $0.10
- Average new car - $610

*Source – The People History: Where People, History and Memories Join Together

EARLY MIGRATION –
LOUISE, MISSISSIPPI TO CHICAGO, ILLINOIS

> *"Having grown up in Chicago, I have often listened with fascination to the stories of those who spent their early years in the South, Mississippi, Arkansas, and Alabama. My father, born in New Orleans, Louisiana, came to Chicago when he was about fifteen years old. He never returned to Louisiana. Never knew how he left or why. Never heard him talk about the experience. Never asked. I do recall my mother telling me, usually after one of my angry outbursts about Northern racial injustice, 'I'm glad you didn't grow up in the South. Those white folks would have killed you.'"*
>
> **Walter M. Perkins**

To be black in Mississippi in 1932 was a tenuous, day-to-day existence. Montgomery recalls, *"Our frame house was called a shotgun house because you could fire a weapon through the front door and the bullet would exit the back door striking nothing in between."*

38

It was, in fact, a two-room house consisting of an all-purpose room, where the three Montgomery brothers slept in the front by the fireplace, on a "tick." The parents slept in the back on a bed. The "tick" had an opening at the top stuffed with cotton, the cash crop on the Mississippi Delta farm where Montgomery was born. Another room was a kitchen toward the back of the house.

Montgomery provides context, *"Our family farm was fully planted with cotton. All family members had houses interspersed among the cotton fields. We all grew fruits and vegetables in our backyard gardens. Each home had an outhouse equipped with a Sears Roebuck catalog for toilet paper. We raised chickens and collected their eggs."*

James Livingston Montgomery and Mildred Virginia Montgomery

Montgomery's father, **James Livingston Montgomery**, and mother, **Mildred Virginia Montgomery**, held the five-member family together. There were three sons: **Leo**, the eldest who was one year older than James; **James**, the middle son; and **Cleon**, the youngest and one year younger than James.

Montgomery recalls that his father *"never finished grammar school. I never saw my father picking cotton. He worked in town for a grocery and meat market owned by a Chinese man whom we knew as Lee Chinaman. I doubt that was his true name."*

Continuing, he says, *"I remember that my dad was the first person in Louise to get a radio, right after rural electrification. We would listen to broadcasts of Joe Louis' fights. Many of our relatives would come."*

Such social events unified blacks across the country, not just in Louise, Mississippi. Recalling this experience Montgomery states, *"One of the earliest limericks I learned was about Joe Louis whipping Max Schmeling. 'White folks, white folks, don't get mad, Joe Louis will whip Max Schmeling's ass.'"*

Back then, stories about blacks suddenly leaving Mississippi and other southern states in the middle of the night were common. The Montgomery family's experience was no different. When he was five or six years old, James woke up one morning to find his father gone. No one would say exactly what happened. In fact, he didn't find out until **1987**, more than **fifty years** later at his father's *"homegoing,"* the events leading up to the night when his father left Louise, Mississippi.

Growing up all he knew was, *"Under cover of darkness, my father stood by the store next to the railroad tracks just as you enter Louise, waiting on a freight train headed to Chicago. It was unclear why he left by a freight train at night. It was clear that he had to leave. My mother would always deflect the questions. I did not pursue the answer."*

Finally, at his father's repast in Montgomery's Chicago home, his father's brother, Uncle William (aka *"Uncle Much"*) told him why *'Dad'* had made such a hasty exit from Mississippi.

> *By the time my dad fled Mississippi he worked as a deliveryman for a white man who owned a laundry and cleaners in* **Yazoo City**. *He would collect the cost of the cleaning services and be paid a percentage. At some point, the owner falsely accused my dad of stealing his money.*

> *Based on the assumption that my dad would not get a fair trial in Mississippi if he had been formally charged, my Uncle Much convinced Dad to go to Chicago. Uncle Much drove Dad to neighboring* **Midnight, Mississippi**, *where he caught the train to Chicago. By this time I was skeptical, but I took Uncle Much at his word. I was happy to get a resolution to a long-term mystery.*

The disciplinarian of the Montgomery family was James' mother, Mildred, whom Montgomery recalls as *"a beautiful, young mother, born in* **Yazoo City, Mississippi**. *She believed in corporal punishment with compassion."*

l-r: James Livingston Montgomery and Mildred Virginia Montgomery, early 1980s

In some detail Montgomery remembers his mother wielding a small switch on him and his two brothers. Once they became teenagers, *"Her weapon of choice became the ominous ironing cord. One time, my father became enraged because of my brother Leo's misconduct, pursuing him with a wooden plank torn from a fence. My mother sprang into action, seizing the plank from my father and telling him to never again lay a hand on her boys."*

After that incident, Mother Mildred became the family's sole disciplinarian.

Montgomery recounts picking cotton with his mother and brothers. *"We would place a long, cotton sack over one shoulder and walk the cotton rows. After the sack was full, or as full as we could carry, we would drag it to the end of a row where it would be taken to town to the cotton gin. We didn't know what happened after that."*

Not surprisingly, his mother was the one who taught the Montgomery brothers good manners and white-folks' protocol. *"She taught us to say 'yes sir' and 'yes ma'am' to adults; and to say 'yes sir' and 'yes ma'am' to white folks, whether they were your elders or not."*

In the rural south in the 1930s, black parents realized that the formal lessons their children learned in school, perhaps paled in importance to the informal lessons they had to learn to survive **rampant racism**, fueled by the mostly unwritten rules of **white supremacy**. Young black children were especially vulnerable because, if not taught, they might not know when they had broken one of the many and varied rules of **white engagement**.

Even now—decades later—Montgomery vividly remembers the lessons learned about race relations from his mother. *"My mother was deathly afraid of white folks. We were warned not to sass white folks for fear of all sorts of bad things happening to you."*

About a year after his father moved to Chicago, he sent for his family after finding work and a place for them to live. His mother went first, followed by the three brothers around 1939.

Several years after arriving in Chicago, Montgomery's mother returned to Mississippi to visit. The family was told that upon arriving she entered a telephone booth to practice saying 'yessum' and 'noome,' and other terms.

This exercise was done to blend in and satisfy the white man's insistence on deference, according to Montgomery. *"I was very upset with her about that, but I kept my opinion to myself. While we lived in Mississippi, I knew she was teaching us the ways of the South so we would be safe from the wrath and racism of whites."*

Historically, this unique duality experienced by African Americans has been well documented by Dr. W.E.B. DuBois and others.

This is the painful reality of having one foot in the white world and the other in one's own world. A sort of dissociative identity disorder, requiring blacks to live on the edge of society, needing acceptance to survive from those who find their very presence unacceptable. And then, hoping to find solace in their world, they discover that those residing in that world are experiencing the same lack of connection in their sense of identity and reality.

Before leaving Mississippi, Mildred Montgomery was a teacher in the colored schools. Completion of her first two years of high school qualified her for that position. The Montgomery brothers began their education early. He recalls his mother teaching at various schools in and around Louise, like Coal Lake. He emphasizes, *"We went to school wherever she taught."*

James' father, however, dropped out of grammar school, which was a common occurrence in those days for blacks living in the rural south. Montgomery remembers with amusement, *"My dad would kid us, claiming he quit school when they tried to get him to spell "taters" with a P."*

Continuing, he recalls his father having a great sense of humor. However, sometimes the family didn't know whether he was joking or serious. *"He would often say, 'When I die, don't bury me. Just burn me up and throw me in the lake.' We were convinced he was joking. When he died, we gave him a great funeral. Mayor Washington spoke, and many friends and relatives attended. Later that night, Uncle Much told me that my dad wanted to be cremated. I would have done so, but we always thought he was kidding."*

CHICAGO HERE WE COME – JAMES D., LEO AND CLEON

After Mildred had joined James Livingston in Chicago, the Montgomery brothers lived with their mother's sister, **Aunt Annie Mae** in Louise. Montgomery explains that about three months later, his mother sent them three brown and green jackets for the trip north. *"My aunt sewed three-by-five cards in each of the jackets. Mine read, 'this is James D. Montgomery. He is going*

42

to Chicago, Illinois. He is getting off at the 63rd Street Station. His mother, Mildred Montgomery, will meet him there.' Similar messages were written for my brothers."

Because this era was before the time of **KFC** or **Harold's Chicken**—the iconic Chicago-based brand—the brothers were gifted with a shoebox filled with fried chicken and homemade biscuits. With that and their suitcases, they made their way to Chicago.

> *We probably rode in the colored section of the train, but that totally escaped my attention. We were leaving a small, cotton-farming town where all our neighbors were members of the family. Life was simple and uncomplicated.*
>
> *Work activity mostly consisted of planting, hoeing, and manually picking cotton before taking our harvest to the cotton gin. At some point every year, each family would get a few dollars for their annual labor.*

Once the Montgomery brothers exited the train in Chicago, the family officially became part of the *Great Migration* of southerners who moved to the North, seeking better lives.

Many scholars cite **1916** as the first year, continuing to about **1970**. Other historical sources reference **1910** to **1930** as **Great Migration I**, when more than **1.6 million southerners** headed north; and **1940 – 1970** as **Great Migration II**.

Between **1910** and **1930**, the black populations in cities like **Chicago, Philadelphia, Detroit, Cleveland**, and **New York City** increased by about **forty percent**.

Before **1916**, few black Chicagoans encouraged their friends and relatives to join them. Even the *Chicago Defender*, which later would become the primary advocate for northward migration, advised black southerners to fight racism in the South rather than seek new homes. *"The Southland is rich and fertile,"* advised Editor Robert Abbott. He and other prominent black Chicagoans saw no advantage in an influx of unemployable men and women likely to become a burden on the community.

*Source – Chicago And The "Great Migration" – James Grossman, Historical Research and Narrative

However, the start of **World War I** in **1916** was a game changer. Northern factories and other employers began losing workers as white Americans rushed to join the military. This forced white employers to recruit, however reluctantly, white women, and even more reluctantly, black men. Remember, the military was still segregated, a situation that would last until **President Harry Truman** issued **Executive Order 9981** on **July 26, 1948**.

It read in relevant part: *"There shall be equality of treatment and opportunity for all persons in the armed forces without regard to race, color, religion or national origin."*

A group called the **Great Migration Centennial Commission** designated 2016 as the one hundredth year of the beginning of the trek from the South to the North, with a series of yearlong events. Also, since 1965, some have noted what they term the *"New Great Migration"* **or reverse migration**, the return of northern blacks to the South.

Chapter 03

CHICAGO, THE CITY THAT WORKS?

"Traveling around I found, up-South and down-South,
it's no different."

Fannie Lou Hamer – Civil Rights Activist

EARLY LIFE IN CHICAGO

Montgomery explains, *"Chicago was drastically different from Louise. I thought it was great. We had central heat, a fireplace. We lived in a brick house instead of a shack, a shotgun house. My Uncle Henry and Aunt Della Parker lived in a nice two-flat building at **62nd and Evans**, near **Cottage Grove**."*

Typical Chicago street scene

Ever become homesick? *"Never."*

As the Montgomery brothers became used to their new surroundings, it was a relief to no longer live in fear of or defer to whites. Perhaps in celebration, they found themselves often throwing stones, or *"chunking"* at the only two white boys who lived in the neighborhood.

Montgomery notes, *"Leo was eight, I was seven and Cleon was six. There was only one white family in the next block. Their two boys kept to themselves. We never saw their parents. They would exit and enter their house through the alley. We never got close enough to learn their names. But, we did join with the other neighborhood kids and throw stones at them as they raced to and from their home."*

There were other adjustments the Montgomery brothers had to make. *"The neighborhood kids made fun of the way my brothers and I spoke. We had a distinct Mississippi accent. For example, we did not pronounce our R's. Court was "cote." Ironically, those who teased us were also southerners whose parents had arrived in Chicago less than a decade before ours. We quickly fixed our dialect."*

The new arrivals also noticed that most of the families had both parents in the household. And all of the parents worked in factories, laundries, and other industries. Many of the women were employed doing housework. There was one plumber on the block, the first black journeyman plumber in Chicago, Mr. Edwards. There was one minister on the block – Rev. Davis. *"He was the first person I met who drove a Cadillac."*

Upon the family's Chicago arrival, the brothers all enrolled in the local elementary school. One incident still fresh in Montgomery's mind after all these years…. *"I was in the fourth grade in the Mississippi school system. When we enrolled at the **Oakland Elementary School on East 40th Street**, I was promptly demoted to second grade. Leo was demoted from fifth to third grade."*

*"Even so, Leo and I managed to graduate at the same time from **Fuller Elementary School**. I went to summer school one year, and earned a double-promotion another year. At some point, we moved across the street, which put us in another school district, requiring us to transfer to Fuller."*

Unlike today, where charges of "child abuse" will quickly send teachers and administrators to the unemployment line, corporal punishment was regularly used during Montgomery's elementary school days to instill discipline.

STRONG WORK ETHIC DEVELOPED EARLY

Asked what contributed to the success and acclaim he has enjoyed as an attorney for the past several decades, Montgomery doesn't hesitate citing early development of a strong work ethic. This work ethic included the rigorous study of opposing lawyers as part of his preparation.

> *At ages twelve and eleven respectively, Leo and I joined the workforce. He worked at the local drug store. I delivered Herald American newspapers in the neighborhood. One of my customers was the legendary **William L. Dawson**, first an alderman, later a congressman, but then, a neighbor. I won a bicycle as a prize while working as a newsboy.*
>
> *Later, I worked in a grocery and market on East 43rd Street, where my father was the butcher. I would stock shelves, kill and pluck chickens, sweep the floor, and wait on customers. I was not a happy camper working in the grocery store.*
>
> *My mother always thought that I was lazy, and maybe I was. I did everything I could to get fired, only to have my dad get me rehired. I was stuck and made the best of a bad situation. I recall that the store's owner and his partner*

48

*were Jewish and spoke Yiddish, which they knew we didn't
understand. Eventually, I learned to decipher the language.*

*Things often got even worse when business was slow. The
owners would take it out on the help yelling, 'Schveep the
floor!' That's when I decided that I would not spend my life
working for anyone, but myself.*

Once in high school, Montgomery found himself again working for the abusive owners. This time he worked for them in a grocery and market that they owned on East 47th Street. Working there all through high school presented him the opportunity to master more Yiddish. After one exchange between the two owners, Montgomery shocked them by responding in their language.

*One Saturday, after working my first week on the job, I
overhear Sam and Joe speaking. Sam said to Joe, "vi fil
gebn di goy?" This statement translates into "how much
are we giving the gentile?" Joe said, "gebn im fuftsik."
This statement translates into "give him fifty." Then, I said,
"No, gebn im zibetsik." Or, make it seventy.*

One would have to be a blooming idiot not to pick up a language I had been exposed to since I was twelve years old.

CHICAGO — FIRST RACIAL ENCOUNTER

Permission granted by Chicago Defender

Unknown stoning victim during 1919 Chicago Race Riot

It didn't take long for the Montgomery family to realize that whites and blacks in Chicago didn't exactly embrace each other. Any amount of travel around the city revealed that, even in the early 1940s, Chicago neighborhoods were rigidly segregated. And, whites didn't hesitate when it came to using violence to protect *"their turf."*

"One of my first encounters with racial violence in Chicago was at age eleven or twelve when my parents allowed us to go to the Oakland Square Theater on 39th and Drexel Boulevard. At that time, Cottage Grove separated the black and white communities. That meant that we had to run from Cottage to Drexel while white kids threw rocks and chased us."

And the racial tension didn't just exist in the inner city.

*Years later, when I attended Wendell Phillips High School, I also experienced racial tension. Three of my classmates and I were selected to go to **Aurora High School** to participate in an Oratorical Declamation Contest. We finished around lunchtime and went to a nearby restaurant to eat. As I led the group into the restaurant, the owner met us at the door loudly proclaiming, 'We don't serve colored people here.'*

Not expecting such a rude reception, I asked a black man on the street where colored people ate in Aurora. He replied, 'At home or at Walgreens.' We found a Walgreens, but because there were no seats available, we boarded the train to Chicago with empty stomachs, but new racial lessons well learned.

Any study of Chicago, at that time, would have revealed a melting pot of ethnic groups all clustered in their neighborhood enclaves. Cross the invisible boundaries, pay the price.

"Chicago developed a reputation as a cauldron of specifically "racial" conflict and violence largely in the twentieth century. The determination of many whites to deny African Americans equal opportunities in employment, housing, and political representation has frequently resulted in sustained violent clashes, particularly during periods of economic crisis or postwar tension."
*Source – Encyclopedia of Chicago

Those who recall the violent and bloody 1919 Chicago race riots that began on **July 27th** might say that the Montgomery brothers, and later the young debaters, got off easy. Racial clashes over public accommodations were common. Some in the black community complained that the Chicago police often openly sided with white aggressors, mostly to the detriment of blacks, who were simply trying to enjoy rights to which they thought they were entitled.

A black teenager going to a *"white beach"* sparked the 1919 riots. The teen somehow drowned. That death led to seven days of rioting. When peace was restored, twenty-three blacks and fifteen whites were dead. Another five hundred and thirty-seven were injured (three hundred and forty-two blacks, one hundred and ninety-five whites). Because Chicago police were ineffective, for various reasons, the Illinois state militia was eventually brought in to restore order.

*Source – Encyclopedia of Chicago

Abraham Lincoln Centre

ABRAHAM LINCOLN CENTRE

At age fourteen or fifteen, Jim Montgomery made a major discovery, one that was to positively influence the rest of his life. And this, at a critical time when teens are discovering themselves and making decisions — good and bad — that will follow them as they transition into adults.

As we well know, some teens come under the influence of gangs and drugs. Others drop out of school, becoming thieves, hustlers or con artists. Sometimes, peers denounce as squares or nerds those students who stay in school, pursue an education and do the right thing. Just as singer **Rick James** said about **cocaine, teen peer pressure** is a **powerful drug**.

No doubt, being raised in a two-parent household helped James make better choices about his future. Still, the streets are a compelling **aphrodisiac**.

Abraham Lincoln Centre was a settlement house at Oakwood Boulevard and Langley Avenue. It was housed in a **Frank Lloyd Wright-designed** eight-story building. *"The Center was dedicated to teaching neighborhood teenagers social skills, music appreciation, acting and the like. It was one of the most influential forces in my life as a teen."*

Lincoln Centre was where the young Montgomery met lifelong friend, **Harry Wilkins**. Wilkins' most vivid early recollection was young James Montgomery's pronounced Mississippi accent. He elaborates:

"We called James 'cunch' because of his strong country accent. Was he from Mississippi, Alabama, or what? He had one heck of an accent. Much later when I found out that he was an attorney, I said, 'what? James?' But, talking to him today, he does not have that accent at all. But he was a country boy. That he was."

Continuing, Wilkins reflected:

"Lincoln Centre as well as a summer camp in Milton Junction, Wisconsin were extremely beneficial to those fortunate enough to attend. I met my lovely wife there. We were married for more than fifty-five years, bless her soul."

Wilkins, now in his eighties, went on to become an engineer and businessman.

"On my seventy-fifth birthday, my son, Tony, and wife, Dorothy, gave me a surprise party and invited James and his lovely wife, Pauline. That was the first time I had seen James in person in a very long time. It is always good to see him. He is a good man."

Successive Executive Directors, **John Green** and **John Griffin**, ran the program at Lincoln Centre. Montgomery notes:

"Mr. Green was a classic tenor. He taught us songs in French and German, as well as English. Mr. Griffin counseled me when I ran into tough times in college. Friday nights were dance nights, ranging from square to ballroom dancing."

Richard Barnett, a prominent West Side political activist, one of **Harold Washington's** key advisors leading up to, during and after his first election as **Chicago's first African American mayor**, is also a lifelong friend of Atty. James D. Montgomery, Sr. He also benefited from all that the Lincoln Centre offered:

"I met Jim when I was five years old. He lived across the street from my cousin Pee Wee at 631 E. Bowen Ave., his first Chicago address. I met Jim when I used to go and play with Pee Wee. We later got to know each other at Abraham Lincoln Centre."

Barnett mostly remembers the influence that John Green had on him, James and other youths in the neighborhood.

> *Mr. Green made sure that you did what you were supposed to do. He was our father away from home. At least he was mine. I would guess that he was Jim's, also.*
>
> *Mr. Green didn't take any stuff. Monday, Tuesday, Wednesday, Thursday... We had something every night. Tuesday night was Classical Music Night. We had two hours of classical music and a half hour of, believe it or not, jazz. If you didn't come for the classics, you could not stay for jazz and dancing.*

Barnett recalls:

"Mr. Green would talk to us about life because many of us, like today, had fathers who did not spend much time with their boys. But, Mr. Green would. He would take us and talk. I maintained a relationship with Mr. Green throughout his life until he died."

Abraham Lincoln Centre was built in 1905, one of the few large Chicago buildings designed by **Frank Lloyd Wright**. Some years ago, it was converted into **Northeastern Illinois University's Carruthers Center for Inner City Studies**. It also housed Abraham Lincoln Centre's not-for-profit organization.

The Wisconsin camp was also important to the future development of inner city youth, allowing them time away from the daily segregated environment of Chicago's South Side in the mid-1940s and early 1950s.

During those days, the young Montgomery was a smart, well-rounded young man. Friends recall him as an athlete, saxophone player and having a good sense of humor. What they all most remember, however, was his intense drive and desire to become a criminal attorney.

The center had a profound effect on James Montgomery. He reflects:

"The center paid for all of these activities. Most of us would not have been able to participate, otherwise. So today, whenever I am called upon to contribute to the center and other such programs; I respond out of gratitude for the benefits I received as a child."

Going further, he notes:

*"My major objective with **philanthropy** has to do with **racism**. It has to do with the plight of the masses of black people in America. You don't have to ask too much for me to give money for something that is going to help young people. Or something that will improve the juvenile justice system. Or the court system. Because, we end up getting the short end of the stick in those places."*

And the philanthropy continued, even after graduating from law school and becoming a successful attorney. Giving back has been a running theme in the lives of both Atty. Montgomery and his wife, Pauline. *"My wife and I have scholarships in the College of Liberal Arts & Sciences that we fund at the University of Illinois. We have scholarships in the law school. That's just out of gratitude for preparing me to make a good living and have a good life. Also, through Trinity United Church of Christ, we offer the James D. Montgomery Academic Scholarship for high school seniors attending college."*

ON TO WENDELL PHILLIPS HIGH SCHOOL — A HISTORIC CHICAGO INSTITUTION

Opening on September 5, 1904, Wendell Phillips High School was the first public high school on Chicago's South Side. African Americans comprised the majority of students at Phillips then, and today. Named for **Wendell Phillips (1811-1884)**, who was both an abolitionist and advocate for Native

Wendell Phillips
High School

Americans, the school has produced a roster of prominent graduates, including James Montgomery and what later became known as the internationally famous **Harlem Globetrotters**. They were initially formed from former Phillips basketball players in the 1920s.

Prominent Alumni Include:

- **Gwendolyn Brooks – Author and first African American to win Pulitzer Prize**
- **Nat King Cole – Renowned jazz singer, and early host of television variety show**
- **Sam Cooke – Famed gospel and later soul singer**
- **Frances Cress Welsing – Psychiatrist, author Isis Papers**
- **George E. Johnson, Sr. – Founder Johnson Products, the first black firm listed on N.Y. Stock Exchange**
- **Dinah Washington – Internationally known jazz singer**
- **Ted "Double Duty" Radcliffe – Baseball Hall of Fame**
- **Marla Gibbs – "Florence" on The Jeffersons**

Today, the school is known as **Wendell Phillips Academy High School**. It should be noted that **Captain Walter Dyett** was assistant music instructor at Phillips before receiving national notoriety as band director at nearby **DuSable High School**.

DuSable High School was responsible for the development of many renowned musicians including saxophonists **Gene "Jug" Ammons, Von Freeman, Eddie Harris** and singer, **Johnny Hartman**.

RAISING YOUNG BLACK MEN

In these **United States of America**, the raising, development, nurturing and preparation of young black men for the adult world has become a blood sport.

54

If you are naïve, faint of heart, lazy or inattentive, don't bother.

If, however, a young, black man manages to make it to his teen years with a firm sense of self, there is hope for success. But, beware of those who would thwart the legitimate aspirations of black youth. Teachers and counselors do not always have the best interests of your children in their hearts or minds, especially if the children are young, black, and male.

Chicago writer Jawanza Kunjufu, in his searing polemic, ***Countering the Conspiracy to Destroy Black Boys***, addressed this issue in a way that made African American families both attentive and uncomfortable.

Educator and **writer Useni Eugene Perkins** in the introduction wrote:

"Human life has always been expendable in a world that is bent on violence and war, and which ignores the social and physical needs of many of its inhabitants. And, there is no better example of this human neglect than in the case of black children or African and African American children."

*Perkins goes on noting, "Brother Jawanza cites the public school as being the most **flagrant institution** which **contributes** to the **destruction** of **African American boys**."*

Some call it benign neglect, others outright racism. This attempt to stomp out the futures of the young, African American man-child. This has happened to many people, including Atty. James Montgomery. It's not an accident.

"By the time I reached my senior year in high school, I wanted to become a trial lawyer. In fact, my 1949 Wendell Phillips High School Yearbook lists my choice to become a lawyer, right under my picture. By then, I had a love of drama and oratory. I had a strong sense of justice and knowing right from wrong. In addition to Thurgood Marshall, I had also come under the influence of Perry Mason. I listened to his show on the radio and knew that he always won."

Becoming a lawyer, of course, meant college, law school and passing the bar. Montgomery's parents, who for various reasons—including the racist times in which they lived—did not finish high school. As a result, they only demanded their sons work hard and graduate from high school. They felt that was sufficient for them to get decent jobs and take care of themselves and families they might have later.

Being self-motivated, young James Montgomery sought advice from his high school counselor.

> *She did not encourage my aspirations. Instead, she impressed me with the great difficulty of getting a college degree and later a law degree. Even as the counselor*

spoke, I thought that it couldn't be that difficult since she had graduated from college.

Although she was Caucasian, at that time in my life, I was not sensitive to the racist expectations that white people had for black people. I was a believer in the American dream. I was convinced from the lessons I learned in Civics and other courses, that in America if you worked hard you could be whatever you wanted to be.

Up to this point, the "American Dream" had been a motivational force, inspiring Montgomery to work hard, do well, and exceed expectations. Now, thanks to this encounter with his high school counselor, and later experiences in college and law school, for the first time he wasn't so sure about his belief in the "American Dream." *"It hit me like a pile of bricks. All of this is nonsense. There is racism everywhere."*

These racist incidents that occurred during Montgomery's formative years of development powered feelings of anger within young Montgomery. Anger that he says stayed with him for many years. *"Anger has been a major part of my life, from the start of law school until this very day. It has moderated a lot, but it's still there. I took the position that I'm going to make this country's promise real. I'm going to make you live up to your so-called American ideal. It's been like trying to climb a mountain without equipment."*

He warns, *"Anger is debilitating to your life. Anger led me to do some of the damnedest things as a lawyer. Anger led me to do some of the damnedest things in my interpersonal relationships with people. Anger became a comfort level for me. Anger sort of snuffed out love and tenderness."*

Leo Montgomery

THE BROTHERS MONTGOMERY —WHO'S ON FIRST?

It's a common occurrence, several children growing up in the same household. Same parents. Same benefits. Same burdens. One experiences off-the-chain success. The others…?

Oh, well.

Not to be critical, but it happens all too often.

In the Montgomery family, James, as the middle child, believed that—in his parents' view—he was third in a three-man race.

*At some point, it was clear to me, as the middle child, that I
was not getting the attention that I wanted in comparison to
Leo, my older brother. He was considered the smartest and
most handsome. And, then, my younger brother, Cleon, was
the baby.*

*So, to catch up with Leo and gain favor with my parents,
I enrolled in summer school in 1945. He was attending
Fuller Elementary and I was going to Douglas. We both
graduated in 1945 and began Phillips that fall. Leo and I
both graduated from Phillips in 1949. Cleon graduated two
years later.*

As it turned out, neither Leo nor Cleon had college plans. Still, Montgomery
felt—at the time—he was third in the *"pecking order."* While the future attorney got busy with his plans to go to college and beyond, older brother Leo
continued working for an uncle, who was in the meat business, before joining
the Marines.

*"I don't have many memories of my younger brother, Cleon, in terms of
the workforce. I know that for a while he worked as a car hop at various
downtown garages. I do remember that he probably became an alcoholic
at an early age. It was clear to me after law school—in the mid-fifties and
later—he was a heavy drinker."*

Apparently a survivor, after living many years in Georgia, Cleon currently re-
sides in Chicago not far from his brother. After years of neglecting his health,
he experienced a massive heart attack and underwent a quadruple bypass,
during which he had a stroke.

Montgomery says:

*When he got out of the hospital, I brought him to Chicago
where he lived with us for about a year until he recovered
and got everything together. He is a loner and loves living
by himself. He is doing fine.*

*My older brother was also an alcoholic for many years, as
was my father who later overcame his addiction. I have experienced drinking problems, as well.*

Unfortunately, brother Leo came to an untimely, tragic end.
When he left the Marines, he became a *'Jack of all trades.'*
*"He could do damn near anything. He did plumbing and heat-
ing; he had mostly mechanical skills. Leo was self-taught."*

I remember that he moved to Detroit and married a high school sweetheart, had a son. Leo and his wife were at war all of the time. I went to visit them one time, and she had gotten after him with a knife. He managed to escape with minimal injuries. He was drinking pretty heavily by then.

Leo Montgomery   Cleon Montgomery

The last thing happened to him at around the age of fifty-one or so. He was working on someone's house and they compensated him with a fistful of money. He stopped by the local tavern to get a drink. He flashed his roll and a pimp put a couple of girls on him. They get in his truck, drive to an isolated location, and mug him. When he resists, they stab him in the leg. Hit him over the head. He bleeds to death.

Chapter 04
COLLEGE DAYS AND BEYOND

"For colored people to acquire learning in this country makes tyrants
quake and tremble in their sandy foundations."

David Walker – Abolitionist

Navigating high school was not difficult. As part of preparing for his life's work, he became involved in drama, argumentation and debate. College, however, was very demanding. Even so, he soon discovered that his already well-developed work ethic enabled him to master even the most challenging college courses.

In 1949 I enrolled at the University of Illinois at Navy Pier in Chicago.

Today, **Navy Pier** is the top tourist destination in Illinois. The giant Ferris wheel, fireworks, trendy restaurants and gift shops attract people from around the world. Many visitors, including Chicagoans, don't realize that Navy Pier used to house a two-year undergraduate college division of the **University of Illinois**, right on the lake front. It operated from **1946** before moving to the newly opened **University of Illinois** at **Chicago Circle** in 1965, a four-year institution.

The Navy Pier facility eventually closed, becoming an entertainment venue and economic engine for the city of Chicago. The two-year institution was opened to serve mostly returning veterans, armed with the **GI Bill** to cover college expenses. Its three divisions included: **Liberal Arts and Sciences, Commerce and Business Administration** and **Engineering**.

The campus has been described as *"the narrowest university in the world, a sideways skyscraper."* In 1953, Montgomery earned his Bachelor of Arts in Political Science, with a minor in Economics, after transferring to the main campus in Urbana-Champaign.

Of his Navy Pier experience, he says:

> *Unfortunately, I had never regularly been around white*
> *people until now. I was shocked the first day in my Rhetoric*
> *class. I was the only black student in the room. To my left,*
> *a white boy met my glance with a grimace. I tossed a few*
> *choice words that I recalled from the 'Hood' and he quickly*
> *turned away.*

> *Fortunately, there were black students in other classes.*
> *They enabled me to reach a comfort level that made college*
> *attendance a happy experience.*

However, an old challenge he believed he had conquered years earlier resurfaced. He thought that he had overcome the nuisance triggered by his lingering southern accent. However, now his speech patterns were southern, mixed with a semi-southern accent, which he learned from his Chicago friends.

> *When called on in class, I would slip into my southern accent,*
> *becoming embarrassed and flustered. I called on my old*
> *friend and counselor, Mr. Griffin, from Abraham Lincoln*
> *Centre. He advised me to study my subject matter until it was*
> *a part of me. This was good advice. I also took every speech*
> *class available including Voice and Articulation where I*
> *learned semantics. By my sophomore year, I was so accom-*
> *plished and confident that I joined the debate team.*

Montgomery became such an accomplished debater, the debate coach, **Dr. Wayne N. Thompson**, named him as a delegate to the **Junior Legislative Assembly**. Later elected **Speaker Pro Tem**, he was the **sole representative of the University of Illinois** and **the only black statewide**.

"We nominated and elected officers much like a legislative body. The experience was a great confidence builder. I was beginning to conclude that my race was somewhat of an advantage in a racist country. Clearly, as a black, anything you say or do gets noticed. Also, the low stereotypical expectations whites have of blacks sometimes inure to your benefit if you are reasonably intelligent."

University of Illinois, Navy Pier Campus (Provided by permission of the University of Illinois.)

Fortunately, the cost of his college education was not a problem for the new college student.

"Tuition was forty dollars a semester. I could purchase used books for much less than that. My work as a scab butcher enabled me to pay for my years at Navy Pier."

Today, the typical college student racks up thousands of dollars of debt in the form of college loans en route to either graduation or withdrawal. It's not unusual for parents to dip into retirement funds to help maintain their children as they pursue a higher education. This pursuit often takes on added significance in the African American family, where their students are often the first to attend college.

Even after graduation, it takes many students years to pay off their loans. Often, recent graduates are unable to find jobs that pay salaries high enough to both pay down debt and live a decent lifestyle. It is with perhaps a touch of nostalgia that Atty. Montgomery recalls his own experience in the mid-fifties.

"I got a helluva education. I received an exceptional education for a little amount of money. Over seven years of undergrad and law school, it started at forty dollars per semester rising to one hundred dollars per semester. It may have been a lot of money then, but I could work and earn that."

MORE BAD COUNSELING

Like many newly-minted college students, the Phillips grad had no idea what awaited him. The fact that he was a recent victim of **counselor abuse** didn't help. He explains, *"Because I didn't have any friends or relatives who had ever attended college, I didn't know what to expect. I believed that I could succeed at anything if I wanted it badly enough."*

What he didn't know and couldn't have known is that he was about to be victimized by another case of **counselor malpractice**. Like doctors who enter the profession not to heal, but to harm and dentists who celebrate the pain of others, counselors who are guilty of malpractice enjoy destroying the dreams of those whom they are hired to help.

And, they are often successful, especially with students who lack confidence and self-esteem. In this case, Atty. Montgomery didn't have to go and find the counselor. She was assigned to discuss his plans and goals.

> *Her name was Dr. Bild. I'll never forget her name, even though I only spoke to her for fifteen minutes many years ago. She glanced at my aptitude test and said, 'You're average in this, below average in that. You're not above average in anything.' By now, I begin doubting that I will realize my dream of becoming a lawyer. But she wasn't done.*

'While your preference test suggests you want to study law, I find that hard to believe. Anyone contemplating the study of the law must be above average in everything. And, I repeat, you're not above average in anything.'

I became even more resigned to forego my dream. She continued, 'I suggest that you try something less taxing like physical education.' I immediately realized that she was just a stupid racist. First, I was a complete klutz. Second, I recognized that she only viewed me as a stereotypical strong, athletically-inclined black man.

I thanked her for the advice and said, 'I'll take a stab at the law anyway.' I, then, promptly left the room. She intended to discourage me. However, her actions inspired me to prove to her and myself that I could be whatever I chose to be.

I have now been a lawyer for more than sixty years.

Knowing that young African Americans repeatedly have similar experiences he advises:

Don't let anyone define who you are. Recognize that many Caucasian people have a perception of black people that is absolutely false and negative. This lady had an expectation that because I was black, I was athletic. Well, I wasn't.

But for the fact that she suggested that I embrace physical education, I probably would have followed her advice because I had no reason not to believe that she had my best interest at heart.

Once settled, the freshman college student discovered that Navy Pier was a great place to meet upwardly mobile African Americans. Some became life-long friends. Many went on to become doctors, engineers, lawyers, college professors, authors, psychiatrists and judges. By contrast, most of his child-hood friends were from families where no premium was put on obtaining a college degree.

NAVY PIER TO URBANA-CHAMPAIGN — REVERSE MIGRATION

"After two and a half years at Navy Pier, I transferred to the University of Illinois in Urbana-Champaign. Culture shock! The twin cities—which comprised about 30,000 people, including 15,000 students at the time—was totally different from my Chicago experience. Racism was much more overt. Challenging racism in its many forms would become my extracurricular activity."

KAPPA ALPHA PSI FOR LIFE

One activity that helped as James Montgomery adjusted to his new campus surroundings was his membership in **Kappa Alpha Psi Fraternity**, one of the famed *"Divine 9"* among **Black Greek** organizations. **Nine founders** on the campus of **Indiana University** in **Bloomington** chartered the **Kappas** on **January 5, 1911**.

Their motto is: ***"Achievement In Every Field of Human Endeavor."*** Their international headquarters is in **Philadelphia**. As the fraternity expanded, the **University of Illinois Chapter, the Beta**, was the second **chartered** on **February 8, 1913**.

James Montgomery pledged Kappa (Alpha Rho) during his second year at Navy Pier. He continued pledging in Urbana-Champaign where he was made in either 1952 or 1953.

> *When I first arrived in Urbana-Champaign, I lived with about fifteen other students in the **Kappa Alpha Psi** fraternity house. It was a large, three-story frame structure with nine or ten rooms. There was also a large dormitory on the second floor where we all slept in bunk beds.*
>
> *We paid about seventy-five dollars a semester for rent. I participated in many events. I still think a lot about that. We even did things together during holidays and other times when school was out of session. The mother of **Don Greenlee**, younger brother of **Sam Greenlee**, author of **The Spook Who Sat by The Door**, and a Kappa, would have us over for Christmas or New Year's Day. She would prepare food, and we would eat and watch the games.*

65

Sam Greenlee, author and
member of Kappa Alpha Psi

*Long after she passed, the
tradition has continued. I have
hosted for the last fifty-plus
years. There are about five or six
of us who still hang around, who
are still alive. Sam Greenlee,
who passed in May, 2014, was
memorialized at the* **DuSable
Museum of African American
History***. Many Kappas attended,
paying their special tribute to
the famed writer.*

The Kappas were one of four Black Greek organizations on campus with
houses for members, two sororities and two fraternities. As expected, there
was substantial co-mingling and partying. Continuing, Montgomery observes:

*"The members, or 'Big Brothers', engaged in continuous hazing of pledges,
including corporal punishment with paddles. Aside from these unpleasantries,
I enjoyed the support and friendship of my fellow pledges and Big Brothers.
After crossing the 'burning sands', I was initiated into the fraternity. Soon
after, I was elected as a neophyte 'Polemarch' or 'President' of the Chapter."*

Longtime Kappa Brother **Ted Manuel** met Montgomery, already a Kappa,
in 1954, when he came to Urbana-Champaign. They became so close that
Manuel later invited him to be an usher at his wedding at Rockefeller Chapel
in 1959. He recalls that hazing was in full force at that time.

*"Things have changed a lot. Hazing, for the most part, has been eliminated.
But, back then, pledges could always count on getting paddled, and Jim was
good at that; oh, boy, was he ever!"*

Manuel graduated from the University of Illinois with a degree in Land Economics (Real Estate). He spent most of his career in the beauty salon industry,
later becoming vice president of Advertising, Sales Promotions and related duties for Revlon's Professional Products Division. He is proud of the fact that he
was one of only two vice presidents in the Division, both African American.

He and Atty. Montgomery have remained active with the Quarter Century
Kappas' Group, those with more than twenty-five years of fraternity service.

*"We would meet for breakfast once a month and have speakers come in to dis-
cuss various topics of interest to the group. Jim would come once in a while.
But, being in demand as a speaker, he showed up less than the rest of us. Of
course, he's on various boards, including the University of Illinois Board of
Trustees. So, he is a pretty busy guy."*

Kappa Alpha Psi group picture

Atty. Montgomery reflects on his undergraduate years at the University of Illinois:

> *Those were some of the happiest experiences of my life. I met black students from all over the state. Some were from dirt-poor ghetto communities like myself. Others came from middle and upper-middle class families. On weekends, we went to the local campus joints, drank beer and caroused. Because we couldn't afford more than one bottle of beer, we bought a half-gallon or two from the liquor store in town. We then slipped it into the beer joint in gym bags. We would continue refilling the single beer bottles that we purchased inside until we ran out.*

The partying continued until the money ran out. *"Dinner became a bowl of chili and extra crackers from Steak 'n Shake. The price was only fifteen cents. I would then buy a Coke from the machine in the Kappa House for a nickel."*

Montgomery discovered he wasn't the only Kappa with a cash flow problem. *"I joined many of my Kappa Brothers and got a meal job at one of the affluent white fraternity houses. We were able to eat lunch and dinner after the members were served."*

Although not foreseeing this kind of situation, temporary as it might be, he realized that sometimes you've just got to do what you've got to do. Everything was moving along until Montgomery ran for and won a seat in the Student Senate. Then, the intensity of his situation increased.

67

The following Sunday morning as I was serving breakfast, white fraternity members derisively said, 'Bring me a cup of coffee senator.' After several such requests, I quit and walked out. Times were tough for the next few weeks until I landed a job in the Illini Union Building's Kaiser dining room. There, I earned enough to pay for all of my meals.

This type of occurrence was one of many instances where my pride got in the way of my best financial interests. Later, when I became an attorney, one of those fraternity members became my law partner for several years. Another was our principal client.

At one point, there were so many of my Kappa Brothers who had meal jobs that one day a white student came to the house asking, 'Is this the waiter fraternity?'

FINISHING UNDERGRADUATE — FINALLY, LAW SCHOOL

Now turning to academics, Montgomery, Sr. decided to major in **Political Science** and minor in **Economics**. These were good decisions because his major provided a solid introduction to **Constitutional Law**, a personal interest of his and also one of the foundations of a sound legal education.

Becoming versed in economics and finances also proved to be a sound decision for the aspiring attorney. Reflecting he says, *"I didn't get a lot out of economics. Although, I had already begun to realize that running a law practice is a business. You need to apply business principles. It took me years to learn the business of the law. Perhaps, I should have majored in business and minored in political science."*

Between his academic life and social life, the young college student stayed busy and productive. However, adjusting to the rural aspects of Urbana-Champaign, coupled with the reality of segregated public facilities, presented significant problems. In fact, he learned that, not too long before he arrived, African Americans were forced to sit in the local theater's balcony. The theater was located only a half a block from the student union.

Also, white barbers would not—and sometimes could not—cut black students' hair. This racist behavior was tolerated at a public, taxpayer-supported university, located in the northern part of the country. While the texture, style, and appearance of the hair of African American women has historically been a source of discussion and some controversy, particularly among whites, the hair of African American men has its issues as well.

Back in the days of segregation, when away from home, African American men often had the additional problem of determining where to go to get a haircut. Sometimes, it was also a problem in the inner city, as well. Even now in some states, including Illinois, the state prohibits felons from getting barber licenses and beautician licenses to work in beauty salons.

Sidney Miller, another Kappa Brother, also attended Navy Pier but met Jim Montgomery at the University of Illinois. He earned his Bachelor's degree in Physical Education in 1954. He later came back and earned a Master's in Health Education in 1958. He first worked as a teacher and track coach for the Chicago Board of Education for about eleven years. He then went to Chicago Teacher's College (Chicago State University), working there for another thirty years, before retiring in 1999.

Miller recalls, *"The issue for us on campus was finding a barbershop without having to go to black barbers in the town of Urbana-Champaign."*

The problem according to Miller:

> *The gentlemen who were black barbers were part-time barbers and full-time waiters on trains that ran through Champaign, going from Chicago to New Orleans and back.*
>
> *White barbers would not cut your hair, saying they needed special tools. This excuse was a tremendous insult to us. Our response was, 'What special tools does a barber need beyond clippers, scissors, and a comb?'*

Montgomery says:

"There wasn't a place at the University of Illinois where you weren't reminded that you were black. There was University-sanctioned housing discrimination. There wasn't enough student housing; so, they had University-approved housing. No student could live there unless approved by the university. And, of course, they all excluded African Americans. So we had to fight, picket and go to war."

Although he still had to complete his last two years of undergraduate study, Montgomery's mind never strayed far from his ultimate goal of being accepted to law school and finally becoming an attorney. And, he was set on the University of Illinois College of Law.

However, now and then, he remembers a conversation that he had with an old friend:

> *Herb Scott, who was a year ahead of me as well as a University of Illinois Political Science major, was one of my best friends. Just before he graduated, he shared a conversation he once had with Dean Albert J. Harno of the University of Illinois' College law school.*

69

> *When Herb discussed his interest in attending the law school, Dean Harno told him that blacks hadn't done well at his law school. He suggested that Herb might want to attend one of the Chicago law schools like Kent or John Marshall. To my surprise, Herb took his advice.*

This incident reminded Montgomery of his previous disastrous encounter with Counselor Bild at Navy Pier. *"I told Herb that I would not ask Dean Harno or anyone else for 'permission' to attend the University of Illinois College of Law. Later, I applied and was admitted."*

It didn't take long for the newly arrived student to become involved in racial politics. The first day on campus he and a colleague from Navy Pier strolled into a pool hall, on the main campus' business street, also one half block from the student union.

As they prepared to select a cue stick, a voice said, *"We don't allow colored boys in here."* Since the students were carrying a pint of whiskey purchased for later consumption at the frat house, they withdrew without protesting.

The experience was so traumatic that he recalls avoiding the pool hall for the next year and a half. Sometime after beginning law school in the fall of 1953, Montgomery learned that the state of Illinois had a *public accommodations law* prohibiting discrimination on the basis of race in public places.

"At that point, what I learned in law school informed me of the historical prevalence of specific race-based exclusion. There is racism when you go to have a drink and the door is locked as you try to enter. When they say, 'Sorry, this is a private club.'"

Chapter 05

LAW SCHOOL
—CLOSER TO THE DREAM

*"An educator in a system of oppression
is either a revolutionary or an oppressor."*

Lerone Bennett – Former Editor, *Ebony Magazine*

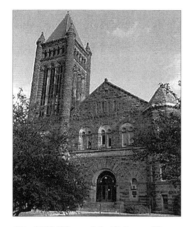

Altgeld Hall housed the College of Law, 1927–1955

But, first, there was the matter of the discriminatory pool hall proprietor. At the time, Montgomery was the only African American enrolled in the law school. As such, he was completely ignored and isolated by both instructors and fellow students. This isolation ignited anger he was already feeling, anger that has continued up to this very day. He says, *"I was a very angry young man; and, still an angry old man, but not as angry."*

Racism is such a peculiar institution, even now. After decades of career success, money, position, and even celebrity—a major figure in the circles in which he moves—the eminent James Montgomery remains angry.

One might wonder, why?

He remembers that as happy as he was to gain admission to law school, he now realizes that the admission into law school did not mean acceptance by his white peers or those faculty member gatekeepers.

"The anger was largely and directly related to rejection pretty much across the board. I couldn't have conversations with white classmates about legal issues discussed in class. You know that's an extremely important part of an education. I never let on that I was feeling sad, not even to myself. The only thing I allowed myself to feel was the anger. It was a terrible, overriding anger that lasted for many years." And, of course, one of the first professors he encountered was Dean Harno, also a criminal law professor. Atty. Montgomery remembers:

73

> *When I raised my hand to answer a question I was ignored.*
> *He never once called on me during the entire semester. As*
> *the only black in the entire law school, I'm sure this wasn't*
> *an accident.*
>
> *By now, I was fully sensitive to racism and determined to*
> *fight and resist it wherever it existed. This old white man*
> *was a relic of the past. I now reflect on the sadness, pain*
> *and defiance I felt at the time. I worry about the future*
> *pain little black children will suffer just because they were*
> *born black.*

Almost any successful or even unsuccessful African American can tell a similar story. Do whites have any sense of the pain they inflict in the name of white supremacy?

Do they in any way suffer from a dynamic sense of insecurity that requires them to have a psychological need to have someone to look down upon? Knowing that these practices are likely to continue, James Montgomery asks, *"I wonder why from generation to generation of white people, the dynamic seems never to change?"*

For whatever reason, his constitutional law teacher treated him royally. Perhaps he had received the memo that racism only made James Montgomery work that much harder to ***"Fight the Power."***

"He gave me the highest grades, called on me in class and valued my contributions to the class. I often wondered if his good treatment was based solely on my scholarship, or another reason. Anyway, I loved his course. I will give him the benefit of the doubt."

Fortunately for him, the legal profession and future clients, the social and academic isolation didn't affect his lifetime desire to become an attorney or his progress as a student.

"I pretty much went about my independent study. The only thing that impeded my academic success was the extracurricular war that I was having with the system. Hours that I could have spent studying, I spent doing things that I considered important. Even so, I graduated with a 3.8 G.P.A. in a 5.0 system, a B-."

The Public Accommodations lawsuit against Urbana-Champaign's Deluxe Pool Room and Bar was the first indication that he was destined to become a lifelong legal activist. And, despite his alienation from the white, racist subculture at the law school, he discovered a new white colleague who helped him stage the legal action.

Donald Page Moore, somewhat of a cultural deviate, having been born and raised in southern, racist, conservative West Virginia, enrolled in the law school in my second semester. Despite his upbringing, he was a self-proclaimed liberal. We easily became friends. Although I came from a Christian background, at the time I was a barely practicing Christian. Don was a professed atheist.

Don once declared he was walking through a public park in West Virginia when he encountered a man on a stoop. The man shouted with conviction, 'Come to God, come to God. And then I came and I've regretted it ever since.' He was a friend to whom I had no difficulty relating.

It, no doubt, was a relief to have someone around who was ostracized almost as much as the lone African American. He had a pockmarked face, irregular receding hairline and wore an old, beat up brown hat.

"The front of the crown had a hole in it from creasing as well as wear and tear. Because he was different, he too was ostracized and the talk of the law school. He and I naturally gravitated to each other and became lifelong friends."

It turned out that despite his quirkiness and odd appearance, Don was a brilliant military veteran. Montgomery found him to be well read on various issues including socialism, racism, and the labor movement.

"Eventually, I told him about my rude introduction to racism at the campus pool hall and bar. We decided to return, and I would ask to be served at the bar, and he would act as a witness. An African American lawyer named John Kemp had just moved to Champaign. We were planning to sue under the state's Public Accommodations Law."

Like others in his class, student Montgomery had come to Urbana-Champaign to study law, not to practice. Yet, here he was embroiled in his first civil action as the litigant. The lawsuit was the first indication that he was destined to use the law in his never-ending fight against the system. This time a system that had denied him his constitutional right to play pool like every other customer of the Deluxe Pool Room and Bar.

Fortunately Atty. Kemp was there to help. It is highly unlikely that student Montgomery would have been able to convince any of the local lawyers to pursue his case.

"We used the black lawyer who had come from Chicago. By the time we filed the suit, the pool hall/restaurant owner backed down. He told the Daily Illini student newspaper, 'Tell Jim Montgomery that he can come in with all of his friends. We haven't allowed black people in this place because it is so small.

We're Christians. We don't discriminate.'"

It sounds like the owner suddenly realized that it was bad business to discriminate. Especially when the subjects of the discriminatory action are affiliated with a state institution with a population much larger than that of Urbana-Champaign, the site of his business.

"That was the start of me learning that the existence of statutory rights allowed you legal standing in a court of law. It was a great learning experience since I had just begun my legal studies."

ACTIVIST ACTIVITIES CONTINUE

Salem Baptist Church in Urbana-Champaign

Salem Baptist Church congregation

It was about this same time that he joined the **youth division** of the **NAACP**. While engaged in a sit-in at a local lunch counter, Montgomery had an experience he would never forget. With others, he sat at a lunch counter, blocking potential customers.

"A waiter handed me a printed business card that read: 'We reserve the right to seat our customers. If God had intended colored people to eat with whites, He would have made them the same color.' We chuckled at the ignorance of the owner and the lengths he went to express his racism."

WHERE ARE THE BLACKS IN URBANA-CHAMPAIGN?

Meanwhile, while ostracized in class and on campus, Montgomery made the joyous discovery that there was a black community living in Urbana-Champaign. Of course, you wouldn't know this unless you ventured off campus.

Historically, that has been the case when black students attend majority white campuses, especially those outside of urban areas. Usually, there is little attempt by the university community to encourage those indigenous African Americans to participate in campus activities.

Often, black students are warned to stay away from the black community. You know, *"It's dangerous you might get beat up or robbed."* Or, worse, *"you might get beat up and robbed."* But, to discover any cultural connection, black students find that they must go *"down the hill"* or *"across the tracks"* to find an authentic black experience away from home.

"There was a vibrant community of black residents in North Champaign. There was a jazz club, barbecue house, and barbershop. It was at this barbershop where black students got haircuts. As mentioned earlier, the barbershop on campus only cut 'white hair.'"

THURGOOD MARSHALL COMES TO URBANA-CHAMPAIGN

Following **Brown I** in 1954, Atty. Thurgood Marshall, now a national legal celebrity, accepted an invitation to come and speak at the University of Illinois law school. Looking back, it is somewhat ironic that an institution that socially isolated its only African American law student during his first year, would then extend an invitation to the country's most celebrated black attorney.

And, it probably comes as no surprise that Jim Montgomery was selected to escort him around the campus. Of course, the campus fathers couldn't have known that they were unknowingly pairing student Montgomery with his hero. His number one reason for aspiring to become an attorney was none other than Thurgood Marshall.

> *Thurgood had just finished the Brown v. Board of Education case. It must have been in fifty-five, because I graduated in fifty-six. At that point, there were one or two additional black students. I guess I was the senior black on the campus.*
>
> *I was elated, because Thurgood Marshall was one of my heroes. I had been involved in learning a lot about some of his Supreme Court cases and issues as an undergrad Political Science major. My whole idea of wanting to be a lawyer was to be like him. A social engineer, that's what Thurgood Marshall called himself and those lawyers who were involved in Civil Rights.*

Part of the campus tour included an introduction to Dean Albert J. Harno of the law school. He recalls:

"It was a strange experience. This racist dean had turned some blacks away from the law school. I took him to visit that dean. It was interesting. The dean was very uncomfortable in the presence of this intelligent, gigantic and popular black man. So, he was very stiff. Thurgood sensed his discomfort, and he sort of changed his...Well, he was bilingual, too. So, he changed how he addressed him. It was interesting to observe."

Chapter 06
FIRST, MARRIAGE
— THEN, DIVORCE

"Real marriage is the sacrificing of your ego, not for the other person, but for the relationship."

Oprah Winfrey – Philanthropist - Entertainer

Under any circumstances, navigating one's way through law school—or any professional school—is complex. Often, even the best-prepared and hardest working scholars don't make it.

Life intervenes and takes you on a different path. Not so with James Montgomery.

While mastering his legal studies and fighting the institutional and individualized racism that he found in Urbana-Champaign, Montgomery regularly returned to Chicago to visit friends and family. It was during that time that he met **Toya Wynn**, soon to become the first Mrs. Montgomery.

"Toya came from a military family and spent time in Germany with her father as a teenager. When I met her, she was attending college in Chicago. She was Catholic. I was Protestant. I didn't realize that this would later define our relationship."

First marriages by young students can be challenging. When they come from diverse religious backgrounds, the marital relationship can become impossible to maintain. And, so it was.

"One time when she came to Champaign, a classmate said 'Jim, you're not going to marry this girl, are you? You know she's Catholic. Your children are going to have to be raised as Catholics.' I said, hell, I'm not marrying a church. I'm marrying her. I had no sensitivity whatever about the impact of a non-Catholic marrying a Catholic. So, I went into it dumb and stupid."

Her family, however, did not have a problem with the situation. He recalls, *"Her grandfather said to me on his sick bed, 'James, don't worry about this Catholicism business. The only reason we became Catholic was because they fed us and gave us clothes during the Depression.' So that wasn't an issue."*

So, he asked, and she accepted his hand in marriage in 1955. They moved to Champaign where Toya finished her senior year at the University of Illinois at

Urbana-Champaign, earning a Bachelor of Arts degree in Education. Before that, Toya had completed the first three years of her undergraduate education at St. Xavier University in Chicago.

Reflecting, Atty. Montgomery says:

"After going together for about a year, year and a half, we just decided to get married. Neither of us had any money. I bought a sweetheart ring for about ten dollars. We found, I guess he was an Episcopal priest to marry us in his home. He gave me a discount, and I only paid him five dollars. So, that was really about young people getting married as they did in those days."

Meanwhile, law student Montgomery was about to become Atty. Montgomery, having graduated from law school in 1956 and engaged in preparing for the bar.

Within two years of being married, Atty. Montgomery and Toya started a young family. Linda and James Jr. were born. He says, *"In many ways, I was a very happy man. I had a family of two beautiful and healthy children and a wife. Once I was admitted to the bar, initially, I was unable from my meager earnings to support my family adequately. However, I was prepared to make the necessary sacrifices. I was used to living with the bare necessities."*

As the only child of a middle-class family, Toya was accustomed to more comfort than her husband could provide at the time. In addition to Toya's father being a career military officer, her mother had a Master's degree in Speech Therapy. Recalling his former in-laws, Atty. Montgomery says, *"Toya was not used to the level of sacrifice to which I was accustomed. They were middle class in every way. This difference in backgrounds soon created problems."*

James D. Montgomery, Jr. and Linda Rose Montgomery

James D. Montgomery, Jr. and Linda Rose Montgomery

80

The problems encountered by the upwardly mobile young couple were not unique. While financial issues are often involved, sometimes couples simply have different views about what marriage is supposed to be about. Once married, they are sometimes rudely reminded that love does not necessarily conquer all.

Elaborating, he says:

"I had no idea what made for a good marriage. I did know how a marriage should not work. The man was supposed to be head of household. The woman should not make all of the decisions, as I perceived my mother did. However, I was committed to my family and to staying married as my parents did, despite the turbulent nature of their marriage."

Money, or the lack of, is often a major factor in whether a young marriage is successful. Low money leads to all sorts of problems. It's difficult to rule as head of household when the money is low. Young lawyers, newly admitted to the bar, are often the victims of low money. And, so it goes.

"There were many times when Toya wanted something we could not afford. She would often have her mother pay for it. I grew to resent her for that. Other times she made large credit purchases in my name and without my knowledge or consent. Those kinds of things gradually led me to stray from my wife and family. I sought love and comfort from other women. Unfortunately, those relationships were unsatisfactory."

Meanwhile, Montgomery graduates from the University of Illinois College of Law in 1956. He prepares for, sits, and passes the state bar exam the first time in November 1956. The young family returns to Chicago and the young lawyer begins practicing law. The marital problems continue.

Chapter 07
LET'S GET TO WORK—PT. I

"Nothing ever comes to one that is worth having,
except as a result of hard work."

Booker T. Washington - Educator

James D. Montgomery, Sr.'s first marriage, and legal career began about the same time, **1955** and **1956**, respectively. His desire to be successful at both would prove to be ambitious, if unrealistic. After all, there are only twenty-four hours in a day and one also has to sleep. In a perfect world, his youthful marriage and fledgling practice might have flourished. But, at that time, the world of **James D. Montgomery, Sr.** was anything but perfect.

The anger he had suppressed for the better part of his young life was ever present and seething at the age of twenty-four. As it would turn out, the twin pressures of a young marriage and developing law career only served to intensify his internal rage.

What now?

He says:

"Needing work, I went to meet **Atty. Joe Clayton**, *a famous criminal attorney, who was also black. During the interview, he said three things to me. One, you don't get rich quick in this business. Two, you've got to work hard. Three, I understand you are a member of Kappa Alpha Psi. You're hired."*

As it turned out, Atty. Montgomery's association with Attorney Joe Clayton was brief—very brief. He explains:

"Soon after I came on board, he had to go to Southern Illinois to the Supreme Court of Illinois. He had an asthma attack. The first hospital he was taken to wouldn't admit him because he was black. He ultimately received treatment elsewhere, but soon died. That was my first experience as a new lawyer."

The young lawyer's next stop was with **Rogers, Strayhorn & Harth**. There, Montgomery was a "book lawyer," which meant he was tasked with doing necessary legal research. It was a great landing for a young attorney eager to learn. **Earl Strayhorn** was a criminal attorney, who later became a judge of the Circuit Court of Cook County. **Jack Rogers**, a real estate specialist, also capped his career as a Cook County Circuit Court judge. **Raymond Harth** focused on divorce law. Montgomery recalls, *"I was the one who sat and held the client's hand in the courthouse. The one who met with the lawyers when they planned strategy."*

Authors' Note: Jack Rogers was married to Jewel Rogers who, at the time, was one of two African American Asst. U.S. Attorneys in Chicago. They were parents of John Rogers, Jr. founder and CEO of Ariel Capital. Jewel and Jack Rogers later divorced. She remarried, becoming Jewel Lafontant. She would also become Ambassador-at-Large in the administration of President George H.W. Bush from 1989-1993.

Montgomery's position at **Rogers, Strayhorn & Harth** was excellent experience for one recently out of law school, trying to learn and earn his way. Thinking back, Montgomery remembers details from two of the early cases with his new employers. *"The first was a state case involving an African American war correspondent accused of the statutory rape of a babysitter."*

Strayhorn and **Claude Holman**, who later became a Chicago alderman, represented the correspondent. Montgomery performed most of the legal research. The client was acquitted.

Another early case was *U.S. v. Julian Black* held in federal court before **Judge Sam Perry**, later a famous jurist. The defendant, in this case, was one **Julian Black**, a realtor, who also operated one of the more lucrative policy (numbers) operations.

Black hired Strayhorn as his local counsel and **George E. C. Hayes**, a famous African American lawyer from D.C. as his principal counsel. Julian Black, well known on Chicago's South Side, had once managed **legendary Heavyweight Champion Joe Louis**. He was also a successful real estate developer. Policy was a side interest.

POLICY PRE-DATED THE STATE LOTTERY

For those unfamiliar, the policy game—though illegal—was a major economic factor in the black community in the 1950s. Though mostly confined to the black part of town, it earned millions for successful operators. It also was a nice tax-free payday for those gambling quarters, maybe dollars who were lucky enough to win.

Eventually the mafia, realizing the huge potential profits being made, forced out black policy operators. They mostly ran things until the FBI began to mount successful prosecutions in the 1970s. Eventually, illegal policy gave way to *"legal Lottery."*

"Julian and his two partners were indicted for tax evasion. I did the legal research. I held his hand. He was a bit impatient. I remember him saying during jury selection–'These are not my peers. None of them can put two quarters to-

84

gether.' This was a great learning experience. So, I began as a support person for the trial lawyers. I also ran to court on small matters."

That case resulted in the acquittal of Julian Black and the conviction of his two partners.

LESSONS LEARNED

In sporting events, casual observers usually only pay attention to wins and losses. This is not true of participants. The same can be said of the legal game. The difference between who wins and loses is often not determined by a slam-dunk opening or closing argument, or a dramatic confession on the witness stand. Often, it hinges on a casual observation, conversation, or the use or knowledge of an obscure law or seldom-used legal strategy.

At one point in the Black trial, D.C. Attorney Hayes tricked a prosecution witness into blurting out that one of Black's partners had admitted paying bribes to the Chicago police. Judge Perry then berated **Prosecutor William Barnett** for allowing prejudicial testimony to be admitted, forcing him to possibly declare a mistrial if so requested by the defense.

However, the defense did not necessarily want a mistrial because the trial was going well.

The judge delayed his decision until the next day, giving the defense team time to strategize. Montgomery reflects:

"We concluded that we did not want a mistrial. There was little direct evidence against Mr. Black. We decided that Hayes should push the motion for a mistrial, while also sending a subliminal message to the judge that we wanted him to deny the motion."

The strategy worked. Montgomery clarifies, *"Attorney Hayes did a masterful job. He preserved our motion, which protected our objection in the case of an appeal."* The trial proceeded. At the close of the government's case, the judge granted the motion for a directed verdict for Black and denied the motion of his partners. The case went to a jury who convicted the two partners. On appeal, the partners were granted a new trial. They then entered into a plea agreement in which they each received two years probation.

"It was my first time working with a trial team and learning the dynamics of collectively developing strategies during a trial. Also, Attorney Hayes helped me learn how to earn the respect of a judge. He knew just how to use his voice and body language to gain both the attention and respect of a trial judge. He was a dynamic presence in the courtroom."

This experience is an early example of Atty. Montgomery studying successful strategic techniques of lawyers, both colleagues and opponents. His ability to not only study successful strategic techniques, but also master them would serve him well throughout his legal career. He would go on to learn a good deal from the three principal attorneys at his law firm.

*"**Jack Rogers** would never answer my questions about substantive law or procedure. He would ask whether I had read the court rules and procedures. Further research would usually answer my questions. **Earl Strayhorn** would always allow me to sit in on trials once I had done the necessary research. **Raymond Harth** was the wordsmith. He was a master at developing memoranda and pleadings using legalese. I later learned to keep it plain and simple."*

Clearly attending law school is one thing and practicing law is something entirely different. He says:

"What you learn in law school is legal theory, as well as how to study and analyze the law. Once you graduate, you must find a place where you can learn from others, learn by doing. Rogers, Strayhorn & Harth was good for me because these guys got involved in some very interesting cases."

Often a new lawyer is armed with nothing but a degree and a license to practice. Without a mentor, entering legal practice can be rough. The business is extremely competitive; so, good luck finding someone to help you, someone from whom to learn.

Recognizing this, Atty. Montgomery offers the following advice to new lawyers:

> *Understand that you've got to work hard. You must do whatever [is] necessary to get the job done thoroughly. That's number one. Number two, don't ask questions about law and procedure until you've reviewed the books and exhausted every avenue. Then, you own it. These principles are important because you will find that lawyers tend to answer questions, whether they know the right answer or not. Third, you must remember that the practice of law is a business, a very difficult business. You must apply business principles to the practice of law. If not, then you will starve to death; the way I did in my early years.*

Many years later, Atty. Montgomery had a gathering at his home, inviting several of those who had mentored him early on and throughout his career. Included were the three lawyers whom he worked for just out of law school, and three other longtime colleagues who had positively influenced his career. After some reflection, he was able to recall one important lesson that he learned from each. All except for retired long-time Judge George Leighton and Raymond Harth are deceased. Atty. Montgomery recounts those lessons.

86

James D. Montgomery, Sr. invited mentors and their significant others for dinner; seated l-r, John W. Rogers, Sr. and R. Eugene Pincham; back row l-r, Gwendolyn Rogers, Adam D. Bourgeois, Sr., Barbara Klein, Earl E. Strayhorn, Raymond E. Harth, Beverly Cook, James D. Montgomery, Sr., and George N. Leighton and Pauline Montgomery.

ADAM D. BOURGEOIS, SR.

"Taught me how to prepare a witness and win a motion to suppress evidence. I recall one time when I had read the law and thought I had the case in hand. But, I had never done anything like that. I didn't know whom the hell I was going to call as a witness. Attorney Bourgeois, whom I had just met, invited me to come and watch him prepare a witness and suppress evidence. I did and later won my motion. I never forgot that. Over the years we developed a strong relationship."

RAYMOND HARTH

"I learned how to plead a case in the old-fashioned manner. In those days, we had some of the damnedest pleadings that you'd ever see. Harth was a master at it. So I learned that skill from him."

GEORGE LEIGHTON

"George was a legal intellectual. He wasn't a great trial lawyer, but very smart. He was a guy who could figure out how to win a case on technicalities. That was what I learned from him."

R. EUGENE PINCHAM

"Probably the greatest mentor for me. Gene was my upstairs neighbor during my first years practicing. I used to go up and have breakfast with him. He liked me because I understood the law pretty well. He used to challenge me. What I learned from him was how to create a theory of defense in a (bad) criminal

case, or any criminal case. A viable theory of defense that was, first, legally viable and, then, second, factually viable."

JACK ROGERS

"I learned that you must charge for your services. Jack tended not to charge for his services. He believed that if you charged and earned more than a highly paid steel worker (in those days), you were gouging the client. I learned that you have to charge. You're in business. You've got to pay rent and bills."

EARL STRAYHORN

"He was a diplomat. I learned diplomacy from him in a courtroom. I learned to deal with and be respectful of the court whether I was happy with what the court was doing or not."

The years 1956 to 1958 were good years for Atty. Montgomery. Things were starting to go well and then he left.

"At that point, I was enjoying the practice of law. I had begun trying many misdemeanor cases on my own and was successful. At that point, Jack Rogers' wife, Jewel, became pregnant with their son, John, Jr."

Having to resign from the U.S. Attorney's office, she was asked to recommend another African American woman as a replacement. The problem? At the time there were few female attorneys in Chicago, white or black.

"She couldn't find a woman to recommend; so, she recommended me."

This opportunity would not seem to have been a good career fit for Atty. Montgomery. After all, he is someone whose lifelong desire to become an attorney had been fueled by a need to force justice on an unjust system.

Assistant U.S. Attorney?

As it turned out, it wasn't a move that he had thought about. It wasn't a move that he wanted to make.

"I told the guys that I didn't want to go to the U.S. Attorney's office. I'm enjoying the practice. However, I need to make more money and would like to be a partner. Laughing, they said 'Jim, if we give you more money, you'll be making more than we are.' That was probably true. It was a nickel and dime business. We were saddled with the garbage of the law business."

Explaining he continued, *"Black folks who had money went to white lawyers. Black folks with very little money went to white lawyers. People with no money came to us."*

So, just as is often the case, the real deal was money, or rather the lack of it.

"I went into the U.S. Attorney's office making about $5,000 a year. That was twice what I was making at my law firm, which was about twice what I earned as a scab butcher while I was in school. That's why I left."

Chapter 08
LET'S GET TO WORK—PT. II

"The job is so fantastic, you don't need a hobby.
The hobby is going to work."

Guion Bluford - Astronaut

Meanwhile, Atty. Montgomery, Sr. proceeds with the next stage of his legal career.

Switching to the prosecutor's office wasn't difficult. The now **Asst. U.S. Atty. Montgomery** appreciated the unlimited investigative resources and advanced technology that enabled him to become a better attorney.

"It was a tremendous learning experience. It wasn't a big deal at all. We had highly trained FBI, Secret Service agents and so forth. We had people who brought you a package that was well put together. Your job was then to structure it with witnesses and so on. I now understood how critical investigative resources are to the success of your case. The transition was not bad. In fact, it was a sea change in the type of practice."

But there was one nagging problem. Something Montgomery's new colleagues noticed right away.

"I didn't think like a prosecutor. I just did my job. That resulted in philosophical and ethical differences with everyone in the office."

Atty. Montgomery lacked a necessary personality trait usually found in successful prosecutors.

He explains, *"Most prosecutors view people (suspects) as 'bad people.' They see things as black or white. I see them as gray."*

So, it bothered him one day when a young, black male suspect, who was charged with selling drugs, showed up in court wearing a bloody shirt. It didn't help that Attorney Gene Pincham was the defense attorney.

Atty. Montgomery remembers that he asked the narcotics agents what happened to the young man. He states:

"The two narcotics agents lied, saying 'He has a bad cold and had a nose bleed.' I later discovered what happened. Of course, Pincham was loaded for bear, ready to suppress all of the drugs they 'found' after beating him up."

91

Later, Montgomery discovered what actually happened from the mouths of the narcotics agents. Once out of court, they didn't feel the need to cover up what happened. After all, he was an Assistant U.S. Attorney. They were on the same side, right?

"I'm having cocktails with the agents one evening in Lake Meadows. We're drinking, and they're telling me the story. And one of them says, 'And that's when we hit him because we couldn't find the drugs.' I said, 'so you did hit him.'"

That's when the challenges of his new job became more practical than philosophical.

"I went straight to the judge and told him what had happened. I said, 'you can grant the motion to suppress (the evidence) because we're not going to contest it.' The judge ignored my request and proceeded with the trial, which resulted in an acquittal. My boss told me to prepare a memorandum for the case record."

By then, DEA officials had discovered what had occurred. They were upset with what Montgomery had done. He recalls:

"I received a letter from the DEA saying I was a lying hothead. That case made me realize that my philosophy, my position on civil liberties, my belief in seeing the world as it is—and not through biased eyes—didn't change because I was working in the U.S. Attorney's office."

His stint at the U.S. Attorney's office lasted about twenty months, until about 1960. Then, he left to pursue the third stage of his still young legal career as a solo attorney. It was at this time while sharing office space with two veteran attorneys, **George Adams** and **Archie Weston**, that he learned a valuable lesson in the art of practicing law.

His arrangement with the two attorneys consisted of mostly sharing space and expenses. Otherwise, he was a solo practitioner. This was a common arrangement in those days, especially among black attorneys.

"I learned that solo is not the best way to practice law. You have no help and all of the responsibility. Occasionally, we would get a case where one lawyer would handle a court call for another. Mostly, we handled our individual business. I learned that black lawyers needed to develop viable partnerships. That way, you are organized and better able to serve clients."

Two cases stand out during this period. The first involved the robbery of a priest, not exactly an easy case to defend.

The parents of a teenage boy hired me to defend him of armed robbery. The victim was a Catholic priest. The tall, rather plump boy was walking in his neighborhood by himself. Suddenly, three or four local toughs drive up and order him into their car. He gets into the car.

After that, they spot a priest walking. Two of the toughs jump from the car and rob the priest at gunpoint. I chose a bench trial, hoping to convince the judge that, given the circumstances, my client was not guilty of a crime.

I was wrong. The judge found everyone in the car accountable and, therefore, guilty.

After that case, Atty. Montgomery did not trust judges for a long time. If he was unsuccessful in resolving the case using pre-trial motions, or if he knew that the prosecutor could not put on a basic (prima facie) case he requested a jury, even in misdemeanor cases. By his estimation, he won about ninety percent of those cases.

"I once tried a case before a jury where my client was charged with stealing a thirty-nine cents Nestles candy bar. I learned my reputation among Chicago police officers was that of a good, cheap lawyer."

Being a good, cheap lawyer was not necessarily a good reputation. But, Montgomery was winning. Next, he was appointed to represent three defendants in a murder case where his lack of experience almost resulted in one of his clients being put to death.

The case had all of the elements of a dream case unless you were a defendant. In fact, there were three defendants. Atty. Montgomery wanted and got the opportunity to defend all three. It didn't dawn on him at the time that defending three defendants in a murder case—or in any case, for that matter—might not be a good idea. But, let's not get too far ahead of the story.

The facts: **Two U.S. Post Office Inspectors** were killed after arresting three black men. They were later charged with stealing a bag of U.S. mail from the South Clark Street mail dock, in addition to murder. **U.S. Commissioner C.S. Bentley Pike** appointed Atty. Montgomery to represent the three defendants who had appeared without counsel. The case was later remanded to the **Cook County Criminal Court**, where the death penalty was available. Atty. Montgomery recalls:

This was a case I wanted. It was tough. It was high profile. I had just enough jury experience to think I was equal to the task. I had little idea just how much I didn't know. Later, it became clear that I shouldn't have represented all three defendants because they had conflicting defenses.

I made the appropriate pre-trial motions with one glaring exception; I did not make a motion to sever the cases for trial. At any rate, the facts of the case had the three men driving an old beater to the mail dock. Once they believed they were not being watched, they scooped up a large mailbag, about two by five feet, and placed it in the back seat of the beater.

The men reportedly then proceeded south to Roosevelt Road. After turning west on Roosevelt, they were pulled over by the two postal inspectors. They were arrested and placed in the back seat of the inspectors' car.

Here is where it gets interesting. Atty. Montgomery picks up the narrative:

One inspector sits in the driver's seat, guarding the prisoners. The second inspector goes to the back seat of the beater to retrieve the mailbag. Realizing he could not lift it by himself, he asks Defendant Wilson to assist him with the bag. After doing so, the inspector instructs Wilson to lock the driver's side while he locks the passenger side. As the inspector slams the door, a gun falls from underneath the dashboard, which he doesn't see. Wilson sees the gun, picks it up, and hides it in his coat sleeve. They both get back into the inspectors' car.

Wilson, now sitting in the right, rear seat raises the gun, points it at the inspectors in the front seat and nervously demands the release of his companions and himself. The inspector in the front passenger seat slowly reaches for his gun. Wilson fires, killing both inspectors.

Not wasting a moment, the three jump out of the car and run, leaving their vehicle at the crime scene. Soon, the police apprehend them.

"After certain 'persuasive techniques,' police officials, led by Detective Frank Pape, wrung a confession out of Wilson. His two companions also confessed. Their role was passive at most, but they still 'confessed.'"

What Montgomery didn't know at the time, but quickly learned was that police often used threats, beatings and various forms of torture to force confessions from black suspects caught on the street, in what were considered **high profile** or **'heater'** crimes.

It turns out that Wilson was beaten with stiff punches to the abdomen. Given his dark complexion, the punches left no signs of marks or bruises.

"I concluded that Wilson did not have a defensible case. I believed his co-defendants had a fighting chance to limit their criminal responsibility to the theft of the mail."

94

Montgomery was about to make the biggest mistake of his brief legal career.

"I entered a 'blind plea.' I later learned that was the worst move I could have made. I had entered a plea without getting a commitment from the judge as to what the sentence would be on a plea of guilty. Much to my embarrassment, I discovered that no competent lawyer would plead someone (in the blind) in a capital case where the defendant faced the death penalty."

He also found out on the back end of his blunder that the judge, **David A. Canel**, was punitive and pro-prosecution. After accepting Wilson's plea, he deferred sentencing until the end of the co-defendants' trials. Despite his mistake, the attorney felt that he still might record a win for the other two defendants.

His ace was an old Illinois case, ***People v. Bongiarno***. Here the co-defendants were held non-accountable for crimes committed by co-defendant Bongiarno. This ruling especially held true when a later crime was separated in time and place. Atty. Montgomery explains:

> *I felt encouraged that I had a plausible defense to the double murder case. At trial, the courtroom was packed. Reporters held down the front rows. Behind them sat the widows of the slain officers, family, and a host of U.S. Postal Inspectors and federal law enforcement officials. I realized that the judge was playing to the media. He conducted himself as the knight in shining armor who would aid the prosecution in bringing justice to the bereaved widows. I was ready for the jury of twelve. The jury had responsibility for imposing sentences in capital cases. I was confident that I could at least keep my clients alive.*

However, Atty. Montgomery had a battle to fight even before he entered the hostile courtroom that day. For some reason, Judge Canel had ordered pat-down searches for everyone entering the court, including attorneys. Atty. Montgomery, knowing neither he nor his clients were likely to gain favor with the judge....

"I refused. A lawyer is an officer of the court and should not be subjected to the indignity of a body search as a condition precedent to entering an American courtroom to defend a client. I so informed the bailiffs, instructing them to advise the judge of my position. They did. When they returned, I didn't know if it was to arrest me, or what. I was escorted to the rear entrance and admitted without a search. The fact that my protest was successful lifted my spirits for the task ahead."

It's good that pre-sentencing spirits were up. They were about to experience what might be described as a rapid plunge.

95

First however, Atty. Montgomery delivered a top-flight closing argument.

"I argued that the two defendants' responsibility for Wilson's conduct ended when they were arrested and placed in custody. There was no evidence that they knew Wilson had a gun or of his plan to shoot his way to freedom."

What next? Well, before we go there, Atty. Montgomery had another little face-off with the judge. At the end of a case like this, it's likely that the losing attorney just wants to have a few words with his clients about the upcoming appeal, wish them good luck, and get the hell out of the courtroom. That would have to wait. There were insults wrapped in praise just waiting to be delivered. Atty. Montgomery provides the details:

"After the case, Judge Canel called me into his chambers. In the presence of his fifteen-year-old son. He said, 'Jim, that was the finest closing argument I've ever heard by a colored lawyer.' I replied, 'Thank you, judge.' But he wasn't done. 'In fact, if I hadn't been looking at you, I wouldn't have known you were colored.' Once again, I offered a weak thank you, immediately wishing that I had shared how I felt about his racist compliment."

At sentencing, apparently unmoved by Atty. Montgomery's eloquent closing, Judge Canel gifted Wilson with not one, but two death sentences. His explanation? Wilson deserved one sentence for each murder. Montgomery was stunned. Already shaken by the verdict, he berated the judge for what he believed was unfair treatment. The other two defendants received twenty and fifty years in prison, respectively.

Believing that the judge was posturing for the benefit of the media, he recalled, *"Before the sentence Canel said that he had consulted his Rabbi and God the night before and was impelled to sentence Wilson to death for each murder. I blasted his decision saying in part that the God he consulted certainly was not the same God I serve."*

On the cutting edge of a contempt charge, Montgomery remembers Canel's response: *"He admonished me, saying, 'No matter who the client or how just the cause, a lawyer should never stoop so low in his advocacy as to disrespect the court.' I responded that I had due respect for the court; it was he for whom I had lost respect."*

Appealing directly to the Illinois Supreme Court, he consulted with Atty. William R. Ming, another well-known Chicago criminal defense attorney, and appeal specialist.

"After briefs were filed and oral arguments had been made, it was clear that I was not going to get any relief."

The problem? Courts frown on attorneys using their trial mistakes as a basis for appeal. That is what the court believed was happening.

"At this point, I decided that further proceedings should be handled by outside counsel. I could best help Wilson as a witness. I received assistance from an excellent lawyer at Kirkland & Ellis, one of the city's top law firms."

The argument presented by Kirkland & Ellis was that Judge Canel had literally tricked Atty. Montgomery into entering a guilty plea by suggesting Wilson would not receive the death penalty. Fortunately, thanks to the outside legal assistance and a courageous **African American judge, James D. Crosson**, the sentence was vacated. The conviction was upheld, and Wilson was resentenced to life in prison.

Atty. Montgomery summarizes saying:

"After two or three years, I overcame one of my first major mistakes as a lawyer. I also learned lessons that would help me in future high-profile cases. Judge Canel was not only a benign racist but also an egocentric prosecution-minded jurist. When he paid me the racist compliment, his fifteen-year-old son observed the racist mindset of his father. I suspect that this is a typical example of how racism is passed on from generation to generation."

And Wilson? Six months later he died from stomach cancer.

These two cases involving the armed robbery of the priest and the murder of the two postal inspectors were important in that they spurred the later development of his legal career. He said:

> *The murder case was especially informative. Not only should I not have used a blind plea, but also I had no concept of the conflict of interest involved. That was my biggest learning experience in that case.*

> *The 'Postal Inspectors' case was the start of me actively seeking out difficult to impossible cases and trying to win them. I did this to prove to myself that I knew what I was doing. That's not how I saw it then. But, that's how I saw it in retrospect.*

ATTORNEY HOLT–DEFENDANT HOLT – JUDGE HOLT

Not usually the way it goes.

In Chicago, there are several routes to becoming a judge in the **Cook County Circuit Court**. Historically, the surest way was to be on good paper with the **Cook County Democratic Committee**. This loyalty assured that you were someone to be trusted when needed. Not too long ago, those wanting judgeships, almost without fail, had to go this route. Several years ago, the process

March 5, 1971, l-r, James D. Montgomery, Sr. and Leo E. Holt

was relaxed somewhat with the creation of sub-circuits, enabling the election of a limited number of jurists who ran without the blessing of a political party.

Generally, if you wish to cap your legal career as a judge, it is highly recommended that you avoid becoming a defendant. Former criminal defense attorney, Leo Holt, later became a highly respected judge; but, as luck would have it, also spent some time as a defendant.

But for the intervention of Atty. Montgomery—who served as Holt's lawyer after he was granted a new trial and would later be Holt's law partner—Attorney Holt might have served some time in jail. Certainly, this is not the best way to end one's legal career.

JUDGE LEO HOLT REWOUND

Judge Holt's unplanned experience as a defendant is an excellent example of what happens all too often in courtrooms, not just in Chicago, but across the country. It demonstrates how circumstances, not evidence, can smear a person as a criminal when—in retrospect—it looks like he just wasn't paying close attention.

One wonders, how often does this happens in our imperfect criminal justice system? How many innocent people are sitting in jail simply because there was no one who knew (or cared) enough to help them secure their release? Unfortunately, although this happened more than fifty years ago, there are some who, no doubt, only remember that the judge was charged, not that he was acquitted.

The following details shed light on what happened to **Attorney Defendant Judge Holt**.

THE FACTS

In **1961**, Atty. Leo E. Holt had completed law school and was two years into his law career. A lengthy article published by the **Chicago Reader's Steve Bogira** in **2004** reported the following:

> *He (Holt) and five other lawyers, two doctors, and a former insurance adjuster were accused of cheating insurance companies out of $20,000 with fake accident claims.*

Holt, his law partner, and one of the doctors went on trial at 26th Street in the courtroom of Judge Alexander Napoli. Holt's co-defendants opted to be tried by a jury. He chose to have Napoli decide his case. The jury acquitted the two co-defendants, and Napoli convicted Holt. Napoli observed for the record that the case against Holt had been weaker than the case against the other two defendants, then sentenced him to one to two years in prison.

After the late Howard Savage persuaded Judge Napoli to grant Holt a new trial, Atty. Montgomery enters the case to defend Holt. He notes:

"Leo was the book man, the court guy. I had become an active member of the **Cook County Bar Association**. *At one of their meetings, Leo Holt came and asked for support for his retrial. At the time, I knew little about the facts of the case. I did know that the case had received some notoriety and that it was perfect as a vehicle to showcase my developing trial skills."*

Indeed the **State of Illinois v. Leo Holt** was a great learning experience on several legal fronts including:

- **Development of a theory of defense**
- **Importance of witness preparation**
- **Importance of avoiding an all-white jury**
- **Realization that law is a business**

Walter Radford had become an expert *"slip-and-fall artist,"* resulting in multiple paydays from unsuspecting insurance companies. These schemes only work when there is collusion between an unscrupulous doctor willing to exaggerate the "injury," and a dishonest lawyer or lawyers willing to take the case and file a claim. Radford had both.

The problem is that Atty. Leo Holt never interviewed or met Mr. Radford. His role was confined to processing the various claims, all of which had different false names.

Radford had a lengthy criminal background, having been in prison several times, including once for murder. He was incredibly wise in how to deal with the criminal justice system. The same could not be said for Atty. Leo Holt who was just starting his legal career.

"I involved Atty. Holt in the preparation of his defense, which was based on four separate indictments. At his first trial, his testimony raised more inferences of his guilt than were warranted by the facts. I helped him develop a full understanding of his **theory of defense**. *That is, the facts you believe will give you a reasonable chance to convince the jury that your client is not guilty."*

99

Shortly after signing on to handle the second trial, Montgomery quickly realized that Holt was the victim of inadequate **witness preparation** at the first trial. This resulted in him failing to directly answer questions, often giving responses that were too long.

"The next few weeks were spent teaching my client how to testify. I pointed out how badly he performed on the witness stand and how that helped get him convicted."

Next, there was the problem of **jury selection**. This trial was taking place in 1961, before the **1964 Civil Rights Act** and the **1965 Voting Rights Act**. Even in Chicago, an astute attorney would not want the burden of an all-white or nearly all-white jury in a case involving a black defendant and black lawyer. Black jurors were often hard to come by back then. Remember, jurors are chosen from a list of eligible voters.

"We selected a jury within a day and a half. Unfortunately, there were few opportunities to select African Americans on the jury. One African American female was picked. I did not like her because of her proper manner of speaking. However, the inclusion of (even one) African American will prevent overt expressions of racism."

At trial, Atty. Holt is called as the first defense witness. Atty. Montgomery remarks:

"I walked him through the steps he took in preparing and filing complaints in each case. He would receive the file from one of his partners who had already interviewed the alleged client. He would not personally interview any of the office's clients. His responsibilities included filing the case and preparing other related paperwork. He never engaged in settlement negotiations."

For his efforts on behalf of the firm's clients who remained anonymous to him, Atty. Holt received a small salary. He testified that not only had he never met Radford, but also he had never met any of the firm's clients. Atty. Montgomery observes:

"[Holt] was a superb witness. He deftly answered each leading question with yes or no answers. After two hours of cross-examination, the prosecutor became so visibly frustrated that he began tugging on the little hair remaining on the perimeter of his scalp."

Atty. Montgomery followed up with a few African American character witnesses before the defense rested. After what seemed much longer, but which was only about ninety minutes, the jury returned a not guilty verdict. Atty. Montgomery's family, including his wife, Toya, and their two children, Linda and James Jr., joined him in celebrating the victory.

Because he wanted to be involved in this case so badly, Montgomery had agreed to work pro bono (free). He says:

> I volunteered, begged and cajoled my way into becoming his pro bono defender. This opportunity came at a time in my life when I was not focused on my profession as a business.
>
> In reflecting, I believe that my personal insecurity was a motivating factor. I felt I had to prove to myself that I was an able lawyer. Also, Atty. Holt was not only a contemporary of mine, but we were both Kappas. It wasn't until years later that I learned of the critical necessity to be compensated for my services.

Before passing in 2014, Judge Holt told the Chicago Reader:

"My mother extracted a promise from my brother and me that we would never embarrass her by going to jail. She was devastated when I was accused of a crime. My greatest regret in life is that she died before I was vindicated."

His unfortunate experience, no doubt, had something to do with the reputation he developed as a judge. Cook County prosecutors were sometimes known to refer to him derisively as *"Let-Em-Go Leo."* This is similar to the treatment famed New York African American Judge Bruce Wright received. He was known as *"Turn-Em-A-Loose Bruce."*

Nevertheless, both jurists demonstrated astute legal knowledge on the bench, including expert knowledge and application of both criminal and constitutional law. *"Holt follows the law meticulously,"* said former Illinois Appellate Justice, R. Eugene Pincham, a longtime friend, and associate. *"The best proof of that is the state's attorneys don't like him."*

Chapter 09

CAN THIS MARRIAGE SURVIVE?

"There will always be curve balls in your life.
Teach your children to thrive in that adversity."

Jeanne Moutoussamy-Ashe - Photographer

"It was probably the most hostile relationship one could imagine. When we were in our tenth year of marriage, I was spending a lot of time developing the law practice, not giving her the time she needed."

The marriage lasted for fifteen years, from 1955 to its dissolution in 1970. Meanwhile, by the time the third child, Lisa, was born, it was in disrepair. In 1967, Lisa was about two years old before Montgomery left home, later filing for divorce. The divorce proceedings lasted somewhere between two to two and a half years or so. These proceedings were occurring while he was still trying to be a father to his three young children as well as build his legal practice.

> *I can't say for certain what triggered the divorce. One night, I came home at some ungodly hour like I frequently did. I went upstairs to go to bed. She got to my male ego. She says 'Why do you come home? You don't want to be here. Why don't you be a man? If you want to leave, then leave!'*
>
> *I said, 'I will. I've applied for an apartment, but it's not ready.' She jumped out of bed and threw all of my stuff out of the closet. I left right then with some of my clothes. The rest were left on the porch. So, that was the breakup.*

Although his parents were never divorced, Montgomery would recall his childhood while going through the dissolution of his first marriage. He comments:

"I don't remember one time in my childhood, or even as an adult, where either of my parents ever said to me, 'James, I love you.' But, I knew that they did. And, I think that I grew up with that same mentality. I'm doing better. I've learned a lot with the second family. But that's just how it was."

If Montgomery and Toya would have had any inkling of the outcome of their marriage, the young couple might have waited until there was more economic and emotional stability in their lives. They may have at least waited until both had started careers. For Montgomery, that would have meant waiting to marry after he successfully completed law school and passed the bar. Then, the marriage might have been a better, more permanent fit.

But they were not and are not alone. **The U.S. Census Bureau reports**:
- **Forty-one percent of first marriages end in divorce**
- **About 876,000 divorces occur in America yearly**
- **Average age of couples going through their first divorce is thirty**

And, for those wondering whether a married couple's residential location figures into the equation, it is a factor. Oklahoma, Arkansas, and Alaska are ranked one, two and three, respectively, in the number of divorces among the fifty states.

The increased pressures brought on by his failing marriage, separation from his three young children, lack of money, and an uncertain future, ultimately forced Montgomery to begin psychiatric therapy. Somewhere around 1969, Atty. Montgomery began the first of what would become two five-year sessions. The first was with a white female and black male team and the second was with the white female.

At the time he was still grappling with his seething feelings of anger, which were mostly caused by his continued personal bout with racism in America.

At the time, if you had asked him who was winning the fight between him and racism, his reluctant answer would have probably been **RACISM!**

Chapter 10
NEXT STEPS

"My position is that we have a good deal to be angry about."

Lorraine Hansberry - Dramatist

Starting in 1966, Atty. Montgomery entered a new phase, developing a partnership with two Jewish lawyers, resulting in **Newman, Kipnis & Montgomery**. At the time, he was still locked in a struggle, trying to save his marriage and maintain his relationship with his three children.

Professionally, he recognized that he still harbored a deep distrust of judges, doing everything possible to avoid them. Often this meant digging deep into his arsenal of pre-trial motions to get evidence suppressed or, if possible, charges dismissed.

"By now, I felt confident in my ability to try difficult cases successfully. But, I remained distrustful of judges and their ability to treat me fairly. I struggled with this burden for about fifteen years."

During this time, with a couple of notable exceptions, his relationship with African American judges was no different than his relationship with white judges.

"For a black lawyer to be nominated, he had to be blessed by the (white) mayor, or the mostly white Democratic Party leadership. This dynamic resulted in black judges often being more predictably biased and pro-prosecution than some white judges."

Also during this period, watching Atty. Montgomery in court was similar to participating in a clinic on legal procedure. He was always thoroughly prepared with a believable theory of defense. This preparation included anticipating every possible element of proof that the prosecution would need to secure a conviction. Atty. Montgomery describes attempting to suppress evidence:

"If the proof required the introduction of physical evidence, then I would seek to suppress the evidence as having been illegally seized. I utilized other technicalities to bar evidence necessary for a conviction. When all else failed, I would usually empanel a jury of twelve unbiased citizens. During this time, I usually won all cases I should have won and many of which I should have lost."

The partnership of **Newman, Kipnis & Montgomery** lasted for about four years, ending in **1970**.

"We were equal partners. Bob Newman attended the University of Illinois College of Law and was a member of the fraternity where I had once worked as a waiter, until my abrupt resignation. Irwin Kipnis and I sometimes went fishing together in Canada."

Although the partnership was progressing, other things were not going well. Atty. Montgomery agrees:

"It was the disintegration of my family life and my struggles with judges that pushed me toward therapy. I wanted to be happy. It was about the time that I sought psychiatric help that my partnership also failed. I concluded that I was the common denominator with all of the relationship failures I was experiencing."

THE GREEN CAR WITH A BLACK DOOR ROBBERY

The best-planned crimes often go wrong when a criminal is not that bright.

Years ago a stickup man held up a bank in the Bronx. In his haste to get away, he ran into a broom closet instead of out of the front door.

Yes, he was arrested.

More recently, there have been reports of perpetrators accidentally leaving picture IDs at the crime scene.

Just like everything else, the successful crime requires careful planning and execution.

Which brings up the question. Why would someone rob a gas station in a green getaway car with a black door?

Atty. Montgomery explains:

"Around 1969, the family of a young man charged with robbing a gas station attendant retained me. The young man, while seated in his car with a rifle across his lap, demanded and received the few dollars the attendant possessed. Then, the young man fled in a green car with a black door."

Instead of going home and parking the car in a garage, or somewhere out of sight, the young man goes to a bar. Soon, the police happened by, saw the car in the parking lot, went inside and inquired as to who was the owner. The owner, now a suspect, spoke up and was promptly arrested and transported to the police station.

Atty. Montgomery admits:

"It was a bad case to defend successfully. Once at trial, I used my usual pre-trial tactics to gain a dismissal, hoping to avoid having to try the case before a judge. At this point, I was about fourteen or fifteen years into my practice. And for fourteen or fifteen years I had distrusted judges. All judges were fascists, and that's how I treated them. Unless I had a sure case, I wouldn't try a case before a judge, always a jury."

Obviously, this was anything but a sure case.

Atty. Montgomery continues:

"So, I'm raising hell and talking about the Constitution. I am railing. And, the judge says, 'Jim, calm down.' I didn't pay the fascist any attention. I continued. He says again, 'Jim, calm down. You're going to have a coronary.' Still, I went on. Finally, he says, 'Jim, calm down; I want to help you.'"

That got the attorney's attention, and he calmed down. Deciding on the spot to trust the judge, Atty. Montgomery opted for a bench trial. Just like the alleged robbery, the trial was short and simple. The prosecutor called the sole eyewitness. The eyewitness testified that he approached the suspect's car and asked what he wanted. The eyewitness would go on to testify that the suspect then pulled a rifle and demanded all of the money, stating, "I gave him the money, and he sped away."

On cross-examination, Montgomery calmly examined the eyewitness:

"The thug who stuck you up, was he six foot four or five foot three? 'I don't know, he was sitting down.' Can you tell me was he bald, redheaded, or wearing an Afro? 'I don't know, he was wearing a hat.' I turned to the judge and said, 'Your honor, I have no further questions of this witness.' And of course, the judge acquitted my presumptively guilty client because of the eyewitness' testimony."

This case had significant implications for Atty. Montgomery's professional and personal life. Far beyond the not guilty finding, it helped him end his comprehensive hatred of all judges. Because of the judicial treatment accorded him in this case, he abandoned his practice of collective disdain for judges. He now evaluated their attitudes toward him on a judge-by-judge, case-by-case basis.

Going forward, this resulted in him putting more mental energy into case preparation, instead of getting worked up about the judge. His career benefited. He states:

"This case and judge dramatically demonstrated to me that everybody is not against you. Everyone is not alike. All of these judges are not necessarily fascist. I've got to figure out how I can operate. I was a control freak. I wanted to control every aspect of the case. That means thorough preparation on the law and facts. It was a tremendous burden. It was also a great educational experience in terms of trying to prevent the state from proving its case, sometimes illegally and unethically."

But, there was still the matter of a fifteen-year-old marriage and three beautiful, growing children.

Atty. Montgomery remembers:

> *I grew up with the notion that a person who needed a psychiatrist was crazy. I was not prepared to acknowledge that I was crazy. Over the past few years, I had fought any sudden or great change in how I dealt with my world.*

> *I had been successful in developing excellent legal skills, utilizing the control mechanisms that avoided risk-taking and the need to view people as individuals. I got along well with juries. I did not want to screw up that small part of my life that was working fairly well.*

Chapter 11

IS THERAPY THE ANSWER?

"Anger is a righteous emotion, almost necessary to your being."

Dr. Martin Luther King, Jr.

Atty. Montgomery was not alone in his thinking about psychiatrists, especially among African Americans. And, even today, don't ever suggest to an African American male that his deck is not entirely full.

But it's true—then and now. Mental-health issues are central to many of the challenges faced by the African American community. The fact that it's not discussed doesn't make it go away.

To be a high profile, black professional in the late sixties, early seventies who sought psychiatric help could be viewed as not only a cry for help, but also an act of courage.

In an **NPR interview** in **2012, Dr. William Lawson** of **Howard University**, an **affiliate** of **Mental Health America**, a major research institute on African American mental issues, stated the following:

"Many African Americans have a negative feeling about or are not even aware of mental health services. They may not be aware of the symptoms of many mental health disorders, or they may believe that to be mentally ill is a sign of weakness or a sign of a character fault."

And, it's true. Although African Americans may choose not to acknowledge the facts, it's true. Even among the general population. In **2005**, the **Illinois Children's Healthcare Foundation** reported:

- **Forty-eight percent of (all) Americans will have a diagnosable psychiatric illness in the course of their lifetime.**

In the case of African Americans, many of the issues related to mental health have a historical base in slavery. Although some believed the election of **President Barack Obama** in 2008 would lead to a benign, post-racial, "Kumbayah," fantasy land existence for blacks, that surely has not happened. Instead, some commentators report that in some ways things have become worse, with all due respect, and through no fault of President Obama. And, now with President Donald Trump, who knows?

Again, Mental Health America reports:

> *Notwithstanding the 2008 election of our first African
> American President, racism continues to have an impact
> on the mental health of African Americans. Negative
> stereotypes and attitudes of rejection have decreased, but
> continue to occur with measurable, adverse consequences.
> Historical and contemporary instances of negative treat-
> ment have led to a mistrust of people in authority who are
> not seen as having the best interests of African Americans
> in mind.*

And, research shows that an **economic thread connects mental health issues, poverty**, and **crime**. So, closure of multiple mental health facilities in
recent years—by the state of Illinois and city of Chicago—may have more
than a little to do with the spike in **street violence, homelessness** and **record
numbers** of **inmates** in **Cook County Jail** who are unable to make bail while
they await trial dates.

This led **Cook County Sheriff, Tom Dart**, who has described **Cook County
Jail** as the state's *"largest mental health provider,"* to say to **CBS News**:

*"People who should be treated in the community with, in some cases, mild men-
tal health issues are not getting any treatment. As a result, they're ending up in
our jail. I can't conceive of anybody saying that that is the best place to treat
someone with a mental illness."*

ATTY. MONTGOMERY, NOW PATIENT MONTGOMERY

After a few years of separation from Toya, Montgomery's first marriage was
legally dissolved in 1970.

Convinced that he needed to do something to restore balance to his life, Atty.
Montgomery called a psychiatrist whom he had met in connection with a case
involving an insanity defense.

*"After a few sessions, I realized that he was more fascinated with my story
than he was helpful. I then found an African American psychiatrist and met
with him twice a week in individual sessions."*

There was also a white, female co-therapist who Atty. Montgomery was
supposed to see twice a month on Mondays. A pattern soon developed of
him always promptly meeting the black therapist, while consistently missing appointments with the white therapist. She finally confronted him, not
believing that he simply forgot about the meetings.

"With her help, I realized that I believed that she was related to my wife's attorney because they had the same last name. Once convinced that there was no relationship, I began keeping appointments."

While trying to resolve the pressures of his personal and professional worlds, Montgomery continued battling his longtime inner demon, anger.

Used to being able to control his work environment, he acknowledges:

"I struggled with therapy. I had difficulty dealing with feelings. My world was logical and organized. I had a view of my world and the people in it that I didn't want to give up."

This struggle led to him making value judgments about others in the therapy group. This approach probably was not a good idea for one who was also seeking answers. Atty. Montgomery recalls thinking to himself on one occasion:

"A drug addict was a bad person. Such a person had no right to challenge me in my group- therapy session. Who did he think he was? I'm Jim Montgomery, a well-educated, practicing trial lawyer!"

Fortunately, as time passed, he lowered some of the barriers he had built around himself and evolved as a person. He describes his transformation:

"I gradually surrendered some of my defenses and began reinventing myself. Over the first five years of therapy, I learned not to place people and judges in neat boxes named 'fascist or ass hole'... I learned to read people and appreciate their uniqueness and differences."

Chapter 12
(BLENDED) FAMILY MATTERS

*"No one family form necessarily provides an environment better
for humans to live or raise children in."*

Johnnetta Cole - Educator

Atty. Montgomery's first marriage dissolved in 1970, and by March of 1971 he would remarry. His new bride, Pauline Creightney, possessed a temperament and upbringing that would serve to not only preserve, but also fortify a family life that Atty. Montgomery desired, but could not navigate or manage alone. She brought some order into a chaotic situation. At the time, there were a total of four children: Montgomery's three children—Linda, James Douglas, Jr., and Lisa—as well as Pauline's daughter, Michelle, from her first marriage.

Pauline Montgomery admits that she was young and naïve for a woman of around thirty years old at the time. However, she had not been raised in America. She was from the West Indies and nurtured in a structured and stern family life.

Wedding Ceremony, March 5, 1971,
l-r: Judge Earl Strayhorn, Archie B. Weston, Sr., James D. Montgomery, Sr., Pauline Montgomery and Pauline's sister, Vivenne

Wedding Ceremony, March 5, 1971,
l-r: James D. Montgomery, Sr. and Pauline Montgomery

She was taught within her upbringing that the husband/father was the head of the household and that no matter what he said or did, the mother must represent that ideology to the children. Pauline Montgomery brought that kind of lifestyle and philosophy to her marriage with Atty. Montgomery.

Mrs. Montgomery describes the order she fostered within the Montgomery household:

"We had to get up at a certain time, we had to have breakfast, we had to plan our day, we had to plan to do certain things during the day, we had to then have lunch. This type of structure aided in the caring of the children. With Linda and Michelle, it worked. On the weekends, the other children would come over to the house. So, we still carried forth the same routine, and it worked to keep them orderly and provide them with a structured environment."

She ensured that the children, while in her care, participated in the upkeep of the home. As a result, the children were taught to perform chores that were age-appropriate.

Initially, Linda, James Douglas, Jr., and Lisa did not know how to refer to Pauline. However, slowly, they started to call her Mom, and she embraced the moniker, relating to them as a mom would.

She loved the children and exhibited love by showering everyone with lots of affection. Her way of demonstrating love proved contagious. Soon, Atty. Montgomery and the children would be hugging and kissing each other quite often.

Significantly, during the Montgomerys' first year of marriage, he asked Michelle, who called him Mr. Montgomery, how she would feel about him adopting her. He recalls:

"[Michelle] was excited; but, then, she went to school, and she said, 'I'm gonna get adopted.' And, some kid said to her, 'What? Are you some kind of an orphan?' So, she came back home crying, 'I don't want to be adopted.'

That event was pivotal in his relationship with Michelle because he consoled her, offering assurance that adoption was good because he loved her and wanted to be her father. This helped Michelle to warm to the idea of being adopted and she began calling him Daddy. The adoption of Michelle was finalized in 1971.

While Mrs. Montgomery primarily attended to the family and home, Atty. Montgomery continued to build his legal practice and attend therapy sessions. Work involved long nights, along with inconsistent income. This reality would last for around the first twenty years of the marriage.

Office Christmas party,
1977 – Montgomery & Holland – 39 S. LaSalle Street – front row: Lisa Montgomery, Mildred
Montgomery, and Michelle Montgomery; Back l-r: Fanny Quarles, Pauline Montgomery, James D.
Montgomery, Sr., Mother of Fanny Quarles, and an administrative assistant.

Also by the early 1970s, Atty. Montgomery's relationship with his white, female therapist had evolved to a point where he trusted her. As a result, he kept
regular office appointments for an hour once or twice each week. Ultimately,
the newly developed trust provided a safe space for him to achieve an emotional and psychological breakthrough. He vividly describes this life-chang-
ing moment:

> *So, one day we were sitting in her office, I have no idea what*
> *we were talking about, but she asked me a question that I*
> *will never forget because it precipitated something. She said,*
> *'Jim, I wonder if that was because you were black.' And my*
> *mind traveled all the way back to 1953-54 when I was in law*
> *school at Illinois. This was a time when I was totally and*
> *completely ignored and rejected by white folks in my class. I*
> *was the only black person at the law school at the time. And,*
> *when I would want to discuss issues after class, they would*
> *just ignore me as though I wasn't there.*

*So, after a while, I got pissed off and just said screw them
and went on about my business. Whenever there was an
exam or something, I'd put on the one suit that I owned,
shine my shoes, and put on a shirt and tie. I'd go to the law
school and see one of those little white boys sitting up there
nervous, and I'd say, 'What are you so nervous about, it's
only a goddamn exam?'*

*After [the therapist] asked me that question, I was cry-
ing like a baby for about fifteen or twenty minutes. When
I finally calmed down, she asked me what was going on,
and I told her; and, she said—and this never hit me—she
said, 'this is the first time in all these many years that you
have allowed yourself to feel the rejection.' And, that was
a break-through for me. I discovered that my anger was a
comfort zone for me; it was a comfort zone in court; it was
a comfort zone at home; it was a comfort zone wherever the
hell I was.*

By the end of 1973, Atty. Montgomery would end his first stint of therapy.
Earlier during the same year, He and Pauline would welcome another child,
a baby girl whom they named Jewel. Seemingly, there was much to celebrate. However, the daily stresses of the blended family combined with Atty.
Montgomery's relentless work schedule took an enormous emotional toll on
Pauline. Often, she contemplated leaving the marriage. Pauline sheds light on
the circumstances during that time:

*The weight of the everyday family and household respon-
sibilities were just awful. I had to pick up and drop off
children from their various activities and commitments. I
had to keep the home. I had to cook. It was just a lot for
me to do; and, even though I knew, intellectually, that he
was developing a business, emotionally, he was not there.
Emotionally, he was not in the family cohesively with
what was going on. You know, he did not want me to work
because he thought I needed to be home to take care of all
of the children and the household affairs; and, I did. And, I
agreed; and, it's a good thing that I didn't work because we
had serious problems.*

At the start of 1975, Atty. Montgomery returned to therapy in an effort to connect with his feelings. He wanted to understand how to identify what he was feeling as well as be able to express what he was feeling to others, especially his family. Atty. Montgomery recalls making a major turnaround with Jewel:

> *Jewel, who was the first of my children with whom I spent time, reading to her and stuff like that, telling her that I love her. I read to her and I remember one of the joys of my life was when she was in college, she called and said, 'Dad, remember the book you used to read to me, Gertrude McFuzz, how did that end?'*

> *Now, this child was writing a composition; and, she was going all the way back to Gertrude McFuzz; 'it was the prettiest girl bird there ever was.' I told her how the story ended and so forth and she must have finished her paper. But, it was sort of getting a handle on feelings, expressing feelings and dealing with anger. It wasn't easy because anger was my way of life. I would come home and cross-examine Pauline after I left the courthouse.*

Political event in the early 1980s, pictured front and center Jilian Montgomery, Jewel Montgomery; far left, Pauline Montgomery, Mayor Harold Washington, James D. Montgomery, Sr., and Lisa Montgomery

l-r: Jilian Montgomery, Mayor Washington, and Jewel Montgomery

In August of 1977, the couple welcomed another baby girl, Jilian.

He remained in therapy until the early 1980s. He left therapy, understanding that he remains a work in progress. Nevertheless, Atty. Montgomery and Pauline agree that he is a lot better with respect to understanding and communicating his feelings. Although, he still retains some of the same instincts as before. He is still working on how to stop holding grudges. He acknowledges that he can hold a grudge for a long time.

For those who may be hesitant about visiting a psychiatrist, maybe the sage advice that Atty. Montgomery gives his children might help end all doubt regarding the benefits:

> *I am a great believer in therapy, and I even tell my children, to this very day, that therapy is a good thing; and, sometimes these issues that you have that are longstanding, that are interfering with your life, you need to go and deal with them. It's like being sick; you go to a doctor when you have a boil on your butt; you go to the psychiatrist when you have a boil in your head.*
>
> *For me, it was a relationship thing. I walked around, as a young lawyer, in the same manner in which Benito Mussolini, who was dictator of Italy, would walk around with his chin up in the air. I used to walk down Washington and LaSalle Streets wearing my little shiny suit, really feeling like I was a piece of poo-poo. Not really liking or knowing who I was. So, all of that was important to me in therapy to learn who I was and to like who I am.*

As of March, 2017, Atty. Montgomery and Pauline Montgomery have been married for forty-six years. They love each other and that is undeniable; it is also apparent that they like each other.

2001, family outing, l-r: Lisa Allen, Michelle Montgomery, James D. Montgomery, Sr., Pauline Montgomery, Jewel Montgomery, and Jilian Montgomery

James D. Montgomery, Sr. and Pauline Montgomery

Chapter 13
COUNCIL WARS I — KIND OF

"The real servant of the people gives more attention to those to be served than to the use that someone may want to make of them."

Carter G. Woodson – Historian - Author

Also in 1967, about the same time he developed a legal partnership with two Jewish lawyers in 1966, **Atty. Montgomery** made the decision to run for political office for the first time. He decided to become a member of the **Chicago City Council**, which at the time was run like a family business by **Mayor Richard J. *"Boss"* Daley**. Becoming the independent **Alderman** of the **21st Ward** was his goal.

The attorney decided to run for alderman because, as a young lawyer, he was fed up with the lack of black representation on the Chicago City Council, as well as how the mayor and his administration treated black people. He wanted to become an alderman in order to bring about positive change for his community and make a difference. Certainly, his motivations for running for alderman were just as naïve as they were noble.

But, this wasn't just any Council contest. It was a bid by a white, Republican incumbent Alderman Samuel Yaksic to maintain his seat in a race against three black challengers, in a ward that was roughly seventy percent black at the time.

Of course, if the specter of race weren't involved, then it wouldn't be Chicago. But this political fray also featured the emerging political interests of the black independent political movement. The role of the **South End Voters Conference** was especially important in this race.

l-r: Chicago Mayor Richard J. Daley and President Lyndon B. Johnson

125

POLITICS – JUST PERMANENT INTERESTS

If there is a **political dictionary**, there is no entry for the word **friend**. In politics, friends evolve depending on the stakes.

Today, it's probably unwise to mention the name of the late **State Senator Charlie Chew** in any discussion about the evolution of **independent black politics** in the city of Chicago.

Chew rose to political power on the tailwinds of the independent black political movement in **1966** when he was elected **Illinois state senator. James Montgomery** was his campaign manager. Initially, Chicago's black independent movement celebrated Chew's victory.

In the 21st Ward race, **Mayor Daley** placed his political and patronage muscle behind **Atty. Wilson Frost**. First, **Atty. Montgomery** was backed by Senator Chew. Then **community activist and journalist**, and, later, **3rd District Congressman, A.A. *"Gus" Savage*** jumped in waving the independent banner, hoping to split the vote and, thereby, force a runoff. It is noted that Montgomery had been a resident of the 21st Ward for about ten years. Savage moved into the ward in order to qualify to run.

Congressman Gus Savage

Then it gets complicated.

Unknown to Candidate Montgomery, behind the scenes, Chew was allying himself with the Daley administration. This alliance included negotiating with **21st Ward Committeeman, Joseph Robicheaux**, who had been given control of patronage in the ward and who was also supported by **Congressman William Dawson**.

Turns out that Robicheaux had his own aldermanic candidate, **Wilson Frost**. Once Dawson threw his support behind Frost in the 21st, Senator Chew abandoned Candidate Montgomery, secretly throwing all of his support behind Frost.

Savage had used much of his political capital with South Side independents, convincing them to support Charlie Chew for the State Senate. When Chew switched sides, it upset the fiery, independent activist as well as others.

He must have realized that three black candidates, two of them independent, would confuse voters, desperate for fresh leadership. In an ***Autobiography of Black Politics*** by **Dempsey Travis**, Savage says:

"Jim Montgomery was an attractive candidate. The South End Conference felt that I was the only person with enough name recognition to possibly beat Jim in the February 28, 1967 race. I beat Montgomery, but lost to Frost by approximately five hundred votes."

Ultimately, Frost won, becoming the new 21st Ward alderman. The cost was the temporary fracturing of the South Side independent political movement.

For now, the question became, 'Who can you trust?' What are you left with when you back a candidate only to have him turn on you in a desperate attempt to gain higher office? Now, with the Daley/Dawson-backed Frost elected, had the ineffective black aldermen, known as the **"Silent Six,"** strengthened their ranks?

Candidate Montgomery came out of the experience somewhat disillusioned. In the courtroom, a deal is a deal. Not that lawyers and judges don't play games. More likely, it's different because, in court, so much is on the record. This type of integrity is in stark contrast to the political arena, where the stage is often a dark corner in a back room with sunglass-wearing participants whispering to each other.

He elaborates:

> *The experience of running for office taught me about the vulnerability of African American political figures to being co-opted by the system. During the aldermanic campaign, I had just finished as the chairman of Charlie Chew's election campaign to the State Legislature. Charlie Chew, the day after we won the primary and beat the mayor's nominee, went straight to Daley's office and cut a deal to become one of his boys. So, that experience let me understand how vulnerable our political officials are to being nullified as true representatives of the people. In retrospect, I am glad that I lost.*

l-r: Dr. Conrad Worrill, Mayor Harold Washington, and Lu Palmer, activist and journalist

Dr. Conrad Worrill, former professor and director of the Jacob Carruthers Center for Inner City Studies, offers this insight:

"I was familiar with the work of Atty. Montgomery from 1961, when he filed the desegregation suit against the Chicago Board of Education. Around 1964 or 1965 I began to hear his name again because he was involved in the

burgeoning Chicago Freedom Movement, which pre-dated Dr. King coming to Chicago.

"I believe that he represented about 1,000 protesters who had marched on City Hall and were arrested for civil disobedience."

The recently retired **Dr. Worrill** is a **noted educator** as well as **political** and **community activist**, having headed the **Black United Front** and been heavily involved in both the **anti-apartheid** and **reparations movements** over the years.

He continues:

"I remember when Jim Montgomery ran for alderman in the 21st Ward; that was very controversial. This was at a time when there was this protracted battle to gain black political representation in Chicago.

*"So, by 1967, the **6th Ward** and **8th Ward** had become predominately black. And blacks were buying homes in the **21st Ward**. So, the African American population was gaining political power in those areas."*

Norman Bacon, a longtime friend of Atty. Montgomery, who also attended **Phillips High School** and **Abraham Lincoln Centre**, vividly recalls his dear comrade's brief foray into electoral politics:

"I went over to his headquarters and volunteered when I realized that Jim was running. I remember driving the car with the loud speaker, urging 21st Ward residents to vote for Jim Montgomery. I was with him at his home the night the final results came in, and we found out that he didn't win. It was a somber time. Jim said he was tired as hell and was going to bed. So, we left."

What was really at play here was the early independent political activity that finally led to **Harold Washington's** election as **Chicago's first black mayor** in **1983**. Many of those living and growing up in Chicago during this time viewed the possibility of a black mayor as something that would never happen.

Mayor Daley who served—many would say ruled—Chicago from **1955 – 1976**, mostly kept black elected officials in line by feeding them **patronage pie**, consisting of a few jobs, a few appointments, a little influence here and there.

Whenever black politicians stepped out of line, whenever they wanted a little more, whenever they wanted respect…Well, remember Ralph Metcalfe?

Congressman William Dawson was perhaps one of the most prominent practitioners of black political patronage in Chicago. Elected to **Congress** in **1942**, he had carved out his own political fiefdom before Daley ever rose to power as mayor of Chicago.

Congressman, First Congressional
District, William L. Dawson

A controversial figure then and seldom discussed now, in **1957** the **Chicago Defender** dismissed Dawson as, *"non-committal, evasive and seldom takes an outspoken stance on anything. Bill Dawson is, by all odds, ultra-conservative."*

He, like many blacks had once been Republican, changing sides in the late 1930s to take advantage of **Roosevelt's New Deal**. Congressman Dawson served for twenty-seven years, until his death in 1970.

WTTW CHICAGO PUBLIC MEDIA archives reveal:

"Dawson effectively used patronage and precinct workers to develop a strong voting bloc that generally gave local, state and national Democratic candidates impressive majority votes. He would eventually control as many as five wards, forming the city's first black political machine."

Chapter 14

KING KILLED
—NATION DERAILED

"Brother, brother, brother there's far too many of you dying..."
Marvin Gaye – Singer – Composer

"'The Coon is dead! The Coon is dead!'
Not understanding, I rolled my window down to hear what a
convertible full of young, white males were shouting my way as I
navigated the Dan Ryan that day."

"'The Coon is dead!'
In response, I shouted something beginning with white, and end-
ing with mother...ers. My life forever changed."

Walter M. Perkins

On **April 4, 1968, Dr. Martin Luther King, Jr.** is **assassinated** in **Memphis, Tennessee** while supporting a group of **striking black Memphis garbage workers**. This was a rare historic moment where everyone recalls, if not the before, then, certainly, the after.

In response to Dr. King's assassination, communities exploded throughout Chicago and the entire nation. Assassination anger collided with love for the departed Dr. King. Many viewed the subsequent burning and looting of mostly white-owned businesses as deserved retribution. **Malcolm** would have said, *"Chickens coming home to roost."*

And, so they did, even today, almost fifty years later, huge commercial and residential gaps remain on the South and West Sides of Chicago. Vacant lots and garbage replaced small businesses, residences, and residents. Lives and dreams not only deferred, but destroyed.

No **food deserts** in 1968, just deserts.

Permission granted by Chicago Defender

l-r: Lyndon B. Johnson and Martin Luther King, Jr.

WEST SIDE ESPECIALLY HARD HIT

Mayor Daley, receiving reports from the field, while ensconced in his fifth floor City Hall perch, was incensed. Not realizing that the black rebellion was the result of years of pent-up resentment — a reaction to long simmering resistance by white racists to legitimate black aspirations—and not just a reaction to the cold-blooded murder of Dr. King, Daley perhaps overreacted.

Dispatching 10,500 policemen, he also received state approval for another 6,700 national guardsmen to blanket the West Side. He then issued the order that no one will ever forget: *"Shoot to kill any arsonist or anyone with a Molotov cocktail in his hand and shoot to maim or cripple anyone looting any stores in our city."*

Atty. Montgomery says:

"There were hundreds of arrests until the community was restored to order. The night and morning hours were characterized by destruction of community businesses, the burning of business establishments, and other buildings."

Much of the activity that had spurred Daley to action occurred along **Madison Street** in **Garfield Park** and **Roosevelt Road** in **Lawndale**. One of the most active community-based organizations in Garfield Park was **The Garfield Organization**. The organization was headed by **Frederick Douglas Andrews**, a **college-educated activist**. The community was heavily populated with former southern migrants and was poor and neglected.

Chicago Mayor Richard J. Daley

Meanwhile, even before King's assassination, the Garfield Organization had gained the attention of the mayor. *"Their activities included picketing, leafleting, and organizing the community at election time,"* Montgomery says.

Continuing:

> *They dealt with community issues and were very critical of Mayor Richard Daley, who viewed the organization as subversive.*
>
> *The Chicago Police Department had a department alternately called 'The Red Squad' or 'The Intelligence Division.' Just before Dr. King's assassination the Police Superintendent James B. Conlisk, Jr., had assigned an undercover officer to infiltrate the organization, which was successfully done. The infiltrator in fact became a trusted member.*

Celebratory event after Garfield Organization trial, starting at third from left: Frederick Douglas Andrews, Pauline Montgomery, and James D. Montgomery, Sr.

Following the infiltration and the *"Shoot to Kill"* order, seven members of the Garfield Organization were arrested, charged with arson and the destruction of property. Bail was set at $100,000 for each defendant, which none were able to make. Someone made a call to **Atty. R. Eugene Pincham** and he came on board. He gathered an expert team of criminal defense specialists, which included **James Montgomery, Sam Adam, Sr., Ed Genson, Earl Strayhorn** and **John Powers Crowley**.

He picks up the narrative:

> *One of the alleged offenders was a photographer who photographed the burning businesses. We had an all-white jury, including a southerner from East Tennessee. Pincham, also from Tennessee, convinced us that whites in East Tennessee were fair people.*

There were several key points in the case which tilted the jury in our favor. None was more crucial than Pincham's cross-examination of the undercover police officer. He used racism as an offensive weapon. 'The day after the riot did a bunch of thugs force two white women from their car in front of the Garfield Organization?' The witness answered, 'Yes.'

Atty. Pincham continuing, 'And did defendant Fats Crawford rescue the women and take them to the police?' 'Yes.'

The next question and answer clinched the case. Pincham asked, 'What were you doing at that time?' 'I was on a ladder draping a black and purple cloth over the organization's door in honor of the death of Dr. King.' 'You did nothing?' 'I was protecting my cover.'

All seven defendants were acquitted. Atty. Montgomery sums up saying:

The jurors chose to identify with defendants who saved two white women, rather than identify with an undercover police officer who did nothing to help them.

We performed a public service, with no expectation of compensation. After the acquittal, we all—lawyers, clients, and the juror from East Tennessee—went over to a local restaurant called Jean's to celebrate.

134

Chapter 15
ACTIVISM—POLITICS—RESPECT

"Many people resented my impatience and honesty. But, I never cared about acceptance, as much as I cared about respect."

**Jackie Robinson – Baseball Player
– Activist – Entrepreneur**

Despite his failed run for the **21st Ward aldermanic seat**, by the late 1960s and early 1970s, Atty. James Montgomery had established himself as a go-to lawyer. He was viewed as someone unafraid of both the legal and political establishments.

He was a preferred barrister for unpopular defendants, a "Movement" lawyer. During this period, his roster of clients included the **Black Panthers,** the **Blackstone Rangers**, later named the **Black P Stone Nation**, and the **El Rukns** as well as various organized crime figures.

Conrad Worrill recalls:

"Over the years, everybody would say 'call Jim' because he did a lot of pro bono cases. His name would come up in the Black Movement in Chicago if we didn't have any money and we needed him. He would always give his advice, or he would find someone to help us."

Dr. Conrad Worrill

Keeping in mind that law is a business, Atty. Montgomery always remembered that he became a lawyer to pursue justice and help people. By this point, these ideals caused personal conflict with what he knew to be an undeniable reality. He says, *"I now understood that law is a servant of the status quo, designed to slow the pace of social change."*

His ongoing battle with judges had mostly been resolved, realizing that all were not out to get him. Still, every day, every hour, every minute in court was a racial confrontation, extending far beyond the usual boundaries of a legal battle.

As a result, he approached each case not just as a lawyer, but also as a black lawyer who was insistent on being respected as such. At various stages, he recalled witnessing the intentional humiliation of black attorneys by racist white judges.

"I refused to be disrespected by any judge before whom I appeared. The first time this was attempted I responded with a loud and firm question asking, 'Did I hear your honor correctly?' The judge choked on his words and backed off, apparently wondering if this nigger was crazy. After several similar encounters, my reputation quickly spread as a crazy nigger who would not tolerate disrespect."

Even so, he had to observe silently when other black attorneys allowed themselves to be disrespected. It especially hurt when the lawyer happened to be one whom Atty. Montgomery himself respected. He describes such an occasion:

> *After adopting the language and bent over stance that Atty. Algonquin J. Calhoun himself would have admired, the paternalistic white judge granted the motion sought by the attorney.*

> *He was apparently satisfied that this black lawyer was sufficiently obsequious and ignorant. I concluded from this experience that I would not willfully behave like an ignorant buffoon to win a motion, or even a case.*

FRED HAMPTON AND THE BLACK PANTHERS

"We expected about twenty Panthers to be in the apartment when the police raided the place. Only two of those black niggers were killed, Fred Hampton and Mark Clark."

FBI Special Agent Gregg York

Tall, articulate, and passionate about the plight of black people, in a different world **Fred Hampton** might have been sent directly from central casting. But, instead, he was a primary target on **FBI Director J. Edgar Hoover's** dartboard of feared **"Black Messiahs."**

How did one become a target? Simply advocate basic human rights for black people. If the media picked up on your story, then that was enough.

Black America is used to the hostile killing of its leaders and emerging leaders at an early age. **Malcolm** and **Martin** were **thirty-nine years old**. **Fred Hampton** was **twenty-one**. History dictates a certain inevitability when you're **black, outspoken**, and **visible**.

Montgomery reflects:

> *I was thinking about how the Fred Hampton situation relates to the recent protests in the Laquan McDonald case. I focused on the fact that when Fred was killed, they indicted the survivors of that alleged shootout. They ultimately dropped the charges after a special federal prosecutor was brought in to investigate.*
>
> *That guy ended up doing everything he could to avoid indicting the murderers. He produced a report that hid the FBI's activities as the instigator of those murders.*

Continuing he notes:

"Historically, from the inception of the Illinois Black Panther Party, the FBI had placed an undercover individual into the organization. He became a part of the leadership and directed all of the intelligence that the FBI needed to oppress and destroy the Black Panther Party."

Considering current conflicts between the Chicago Police Department, other departments, and black communities across the country, Atty. Montgomery says:

"People should better understand history before they call for a federal prosecutor and investigations by the Department of Justice. This is what happened in the Panther case. Instead, there should be a call for appointment of an independent special prosecutor."

Continuing, the longtime civil rights attorney explains:

"The special prosecutor would be appointed by the Chief Judge of the Criminal Court. That's exactly what we did in 1970 when they were investigating countywide. The results were the indictments of a couple of assistant state's attorneys and some police officers. They were acquitted, but at least the special prosecutor was independent. He did a wonderful job of putting a team together and getting indictments."

Reliable reports and testimony from survivors and eyewitnesses of the **December 4, 1969** raid that killed **Illinois Black Panthers Fred Hampton** and **Mark Clark** indicate that Hampton was asleep at the time.

Most people are asleep at **4:45 a. m.**

Fred Hampton was everything that the white power structure despised, as it turns out, not just in Chicago, but all the way to Washington, D.C. Born in 1948, he was raised in **Maywood**, a suburb west of Chicago. An excellent student and athlete, he once dreamed of playing center field for the **New York Yankees**.

He graduated from **Proviso East High School in 1966** before enrolling at **Triton Junior College**, where he majored in **pre-law**. His early interest in the law was important for his involvement with both the **Youth Council of the NAACP (West Suburban Branch)** and the **Illinois Black Panthers**, which he later led before his untimely assassination.

Much has been written about the **December 4, 1969** raid—executed by the **FBI, Chicago Police**, and the **Cook County State's Attorney's office** under the direction of **Cook County State's Attorney**, Edward Hanrahan—and the killing of **Hampton** and **Clark**.

The subsequent official cover-up and findings that most of the shootings were into the house, with no more than two shots coming from inside the apartment, has been heavily documented over the years.

Panthers described the incident as a *"shoot-in, not a shoot-out."* A six-person panel conducted an inquest in **January, 1970** finding the deaths of **Hampton** and **Clark** to be *"justifiable homicide."*

It wasn't until **1977** that the **U.S. Justice Department**, bowing to the demands of blacks, liberals and others concerned about the raid, killings and cover up conducted a **grand jury** hearing.

Atty. Montgomery recalls:

> *The feds called witnesses before the grand jury in this so-called federal investigation. At the end, they didn't indict the police, didn't indict the state's attorney.*
>
> *They didn't indict anybody. They simply gave a report—a grand jury report—which was benign. They also completely covered up the FBI's participation in the murders of Fred Hampton and Mark Clark. You have to be careful with the feds.*

Montgomery was one of the plaintiffs' lawyers in the **$47.7 million** civil suit filed in 1970 targeting twenty-eight people, including Hanrahan and other federal, city and county representatives.

He represented **Deborah Johnson**—Hampton's fiancée and one of the survivors of the shoot-in—who was eight months pregnant at the time and later gave birth to **Fred Hampton, Jr.**

Atty. Montgomery discusses his involvement with the case:

> *Shortly after the murders, a blue-ribbon coroner's jury was empaneled to determine the cause and means of Fred and Mark's deaths. I represented Deborah Johnson, Fred's de facto widow, who, soon after Fred's murder, would give birth to their son. The People's Law Office represented the Hampton family and the remaining survivors of the raid.*
>
> *Initially, Mark Clark's family was represented by the late Cornelius Toole. At some point during the inquest, Toole referred the Clark family to me. I entered into a contingent fee contract with the family to represent their interests at the inquest and any civil damages arising out of Mark's murder. After the inquest and criminal matters were resolved, the lawyers from the People's Law Office persuaded the Clark family to fire me.*
>
> *I was left with just one client, Deborah Johnson, who had sustained no physical injuries during the raid. I, therefore, had no plans to pursue the civil matter, leaving the entire group to the People's Law Office.*
>
> *However, the lawyers with the People's Law Office did not have any experience in trying cases. Also, they wanted to have a black lawyer involved in the case. So, initially, they went and got the NAACP to hire Herbert Reid, the distinguished professor of law from Howard University. Professor Reid agreed to help, but, due to health issues, could not take the stress of total involvement.*
>
> *After that, the same lawyers came to urge me to join in the trial; I agreed. My primary reason for agreeing was to get back at them for alienating my client from me. In addition, I entered into a contract with Deborah Johnson and the Hampton family for a fifty percent contingency fee for any award to Deborah Johnson, Fred's son, and Mr. and Mrs. Hampton.*

141

Having a relationship with those lawyers was a virtual disaster because we had different perspectives in terms of what we were trying to accomplish. I asked them one night when we were fighting after court, 'What do you expect to achieve by calling the judge an old fuddy-duddy and by calling him out of his name and getting him to chew you out in front of the jury? What do you hope to gain?' I asked them, 'What do you expect these people to get as a recovery in the event that we are successful in this case?' One of them said, '$50,000.' In response, I said, 'That's your problem.'

When we ultimately settled the case, the lawyers from the People's Law Office induced the Hampton family and Deborah to challenge my fee. During the contested fee hearing, we compromised and I received thirty-six percent of the $900,000 awarded to the Hamptons, Deborah, and Fred's son.

This is why I often say that I agreed to pursue the civil case for the wrong reason, namely, payback.

That case wound its way through the court system before finally being settled in 1982. The three governmental entities agreed to pay $600,000 each to a group of nine plaintiffs including Hampton and Clark's mothers.

Over the years, Fred Hampton's story has grown to almost mythic proportions. There is no middle ground. He's either loved or despised. Despised by those still concerned about the rise of a *"Black Messiah."* Loved by those who seek to pick up the justice baton and finally fall across the finish line of racial equality.

It's disturbing when people know more about the circumstances of your death than the circumstances of your life.

Few know that at the same time J. Edgar Hoover was trying to pit the Black Panthers and Chicago's street gangs against each other, Fred Hampton was busy negotiating a non-aggression pact among the groups, seeking peace in the hood.

Even fewer know that, in **May, 1969**, **Hampton** reportedly announced the formation of a **Rainbow Coalition**. This organization was a multi-racial coalition that he helped organize that included the **Black Panther Party, Young Lords, Students for a Democratic Society,** and others.

We are left to wonder where a **Fred Hampton**, unmolested by various governmental entities, might have taken his people.

He said:

"So we say – we always say in the Black Panther Party that they can do anything they want to us. We might not be back. I might be in jail. I might be anywhere. But when I leave, you'll remember I said, with the last words on my lips, that I am a revolutionary. And, you are going to have to keep on saying that. You're going to have to say that I am a proletariat, I am the people."

*Source — Excerpt from **Democracy Now!** in recognition of the then fortieth anniversary of his murder.

Those wanting to know more about this historic event should read:

"The Assassination of Fred Hampton: How the FBI and the Chicago Police Murdered a Black Panther" by Jeffrey Haas

October 20–23, 2016 were set aside to commemorate the fiftieth anniversary of the Black Panther Party. Their media image focused on the wielding of weapons and violence. The real historical record reveals that more often than not, they were the victims of violence, not the perpetrators. Advocating self-defense is far different than advocating violence.

A review of their **Ten-Point Platform and Program** documents that the Black Panther Party was an **active advocate** of **community building**. *"Black Power"* was an attempt to gain the power necessary for African Americans to build and fortify the communities where they lived and worked.

For example: Points 1, 2, 4, 5, and 7

What We Want – What We Believe

1. We want freedom. We want Power to determine the destiny of our Black and Oppressed Communities.

2. We want full Employment for our People.

4. We want decent Housing, fit for shelter of Human Beings.

5. We want decent Education for our People that Exposes the true nature of this decadent American society. We want Education that teaches us our true History and our Role in the present-day society.

7. We want an immediate end to **POLICE BRUTALITY** and **MUR-DER** of Black People, other people of color, all oppressed people inside the United States.

*Source – History Matters

Atty. Montgomery makes the following observation about the Black Panther Party:

"The Black Panther Party consisted of some high-quality people. People like Congressman Bobby Rush, who was second in command for the Illinois Chapter of the Black Panther Party. These individuals would go on to professional and/or political careers."

JEFF FORT

Watching the news as a bulldozer destroyed an old movie theater at **3947 S. Drexel**, some believed this was a mistake, but didn't know why.

Now we know.

The **Oakland Square Theater** was important, first as the movie house attended by Jim Montgomery, his brothers and friends when he came to Chicago. At that time, in the forties and fifties it was an important entertainment and cultural entity in the neighborhood. Many years after it closed down it became the headquarters for the El Rukns, headed by Jeff Fort, purchased by the group at a tax sale.

Oakland Square Theater

At the time of the theater's demolition in 1990 (other sources cite 1989), covered on the evening news in Chicago, the U.S. Attorney's office announced the demise of the El Rukns. In retrospect, what the demolition accomplished was the beginning of the end of the organized top-down corporate leadership structure symbolized by Chicago youth gangs in the fifties, sixties, and seventies. These were organizations where the leaders were known by their first names, Jeff, Bobby, Larry and David.

Today, smaller, more loosely organized groups have replaced the tightly run structures of the past. The corporate structure and accountability no longer exist.

At some point the lives of Montgomery and Fort intersected, and the attorney represented him and his colleagues several times in the 1970s.

"I represented Jeff Fort successfully on three occasions," Montgomery recalls.

There are only a handful of people who are universally recognized by their first name …**Miles, Duke, Harold, Billie, Count, Prince**…**Jeff**.

This statement was especially true in Chicago during the **sixties, seventies, eighties** and even beyond. When you said **Jeff**, everyone knew of whom you spoke. It was the early 1970s when **Atty. James Montgomery** first met **Jeff Fort**. Later, he would represent the organization, then the **Blackstone Rangers**, in several high-profile police shooting cases.

Chicago Magazine, in a **November, 1988**, article somewhat colorfully recounts when the two men first met:

Montgomery says:

"One day, I held an impromptu press conference on the courthouse steps lashing out at the white establishment, following a court case. Afterward, I was approached by two young black men. 'Jim, you hate these motherfuckers as much as we do,' Jeff Fort said. 'Why don't you represent us?'"

And so he did begin to represent the organization, as it transformed from the **Blackstone Rangers** to the **Black P Stone Nation**, and finally the **El Rukns**.

He states:

> For the next few years from 1969 until about 1975. I spent much of my time trying felony cases, including murder cases, for the 'Main 21,' leaders of the Black P Stone Nation. Originally, the wealthy son of a former General Motors CEO paid a $5,000 monthly retainer to a white law firm.
>
> When the benefactor learned that they had been terminated, he stopped funding the Main 21's defense. Thereafter, I received a combination of coin and paper currency monthly, which amounted to about $2,000 to provide services.

One of the first major cases undertaken by **Atty. Montgomery** during this time was the trial for the murder of **Chicago Police Officer James Alfano** who was shot to death on **August 13, 1970**.

*"Alfano was a Chicago police officer assigned to the **Gang Intelligence Unit**. He was seated in the rear seat of an unmarked squad car traveling down an alley about a block from the Nation's headquarters. Shots rang out from*

behind the vehicle. One shot from a 30/30 Carbine rifle penetrated the trunk entering Officer Alfano's back. He died almost instantly."

Shortly afterward seven members of the *"Main 21"* were indicted for murder and conspiracy to commit murder. The shooting occurred near the historic Southmoor Hotel at 6646 S. Stony Island, which had recently been closed down. It was near the headquarters of the Black P Stone Nation, drawing a good deal of police scrutiny and traffic. At one point, the abandoned Southmoor became headquarters of the Black P Stone Nation.

On the night in question, a three-man gang unit was patrolling the area on orders from police headquarters. Alfano was sitting in the back seat. According to trial testimony by Officer Thomas Donahue, a front seat passenger, the officers encountered debris blocking their way as they drove through an alley behind the hotel. Detective Richard Crowley was driving. He reportedly backed out of the alley and entered another section of the alley, encountering another blockade, including a stuffed chair.

In an article by *Chicago Tribune* Reporter Philip Caputo, Donahue testified:

"Crowley started to push it aside with the auto. I heard a loud boom, followed by semi-automatic fire. I then heard Alfano cry out, 'Oh my God, I'm dying.'"

The officer, wounded in the back and stomach, died three days later in Billings Hospital. At trial, **Judge Louis B. Garippo, Jr.** presided.
*Source – Chicago Tribune

Atty. Montgomery says:

> *Their headquarters were right at 67th Street at Blackstone or thereabouts. The police raided the place and took everybody down. For several weeks they interrogated people, ending up indicting seven members of the Black P Stone Nation. When the indictment came down, I put together a team of lawyers to represent the individual defendants.*

> *Included were Eugene Pincham, my favorite co-counsel, Sam Adam, Sr., Leo Holt, Earl E. Strayhorn, and Ed Genson, a new lawyer and the junior counsel at the table.*

Montgomery recalls, *"Within minutes of the shooting, Gang Intelligence Officers raided the Nation's headquarters, rounding up a number of gang members and taking them to police headquarters, then located at 1121 S. State Street. I was alerted immediately and received regular reports from members who had been interrogated and released."*

Continuing, *"Some reported being held out of windows by their heels. Others reported being struck on the head with large telephone books, or having their heads thrust into the toilet. Soon afterward seven gang members were arrested and charged with murder and conspiracy to commit murder."*

"THE DEATH PENALTY IS TOO GOOD FOR THEM"

One thing that makes the law so fascinating and interesting is both its unpredictability and its inevitability. No matter the evidence, or how good or bad the trial is conducted, it is dangerous to predict the outcome.

Even afterward, the appeals process can, and often does, drag on for years, either confirming or nullifying the original verdict. Thankfully, once it's over, it's over, the law against **double jeopardy** forever preventing the same charges from being brought against the same defendant.

Before you get to that point, however, there is the little matter of keeping those who might be biased against your client(s), out of the jury box.

In this case, even with the stellar defense team in place, the prejudiced juror didn't show his hand until the end of the trial.

Atty. Montgomery explains:

> This was a case involving some of the most unpopular people in the world, charged with the most unpopular crime you could imagine. Even so, we were able to gain an acquittal.
>
> The trial lasted about a month, after taking about a week to select the jury. They were seeking the death penalty because it was the murder of a police officer. We selected a dozen jurors, including one or two African Americans. We also picked a couple of alternates, including a black man with community roots. Because of illness or family issues, both alternates ended up sitting as jurors.
>
> The black man was the last alternate selected. We simply picked him without questioning, an almost fatal omission.

At the end of each day, the team of attorneys gathered at Atty. Pincham's home to plan the next day's strategy.

Continuing, Montgomery recalls:

"The jury was only out for three days. It turned out they would have acquitted the first day, but for one holdout, which turned out to be the black man who was originally an alternate. During deliberations, he reportedly said, 'The death penalty is too good for them.' He was finally persuaded to vote with the others."

147

This case and the outcome provide excellent insights into the unpredictability of the criminal justice system. High profile case...police on one side...gang members on the other ...top-level defense team...hostile juror... But, the case turns not on solid evidence or eyewitness testimony, but on a key courtroom misidentification and an unreliable witness.

Atty. Montgomery picks up the story:

> The murder weapon, some kind of a deer rifle, was found behind a building on the South Side. The prosecution called a female witness who lived in the building. She testified that two of the defendants William Throop and Charles Edward Bey said, 'You should go in the house. There's going to be some shooting out here.'
>
> Throop was a very tall, dark-complexioned gentleman. When asked to identify him, she looked around the courtroom before pointing to Tony Carter, my client, who happened to be the shortest guy in the group. I said 'Tony, stand up. Let the record show that the person she identified is Tony Carter.'

That was the first major problem with the prosecution's case. Atty. Montgomery then recounts the second major reason that he and his legal team won an acquittal in this difficult case. It seems there was a key witness who kept changing his story.

> A person who turned out to be a key eyewitness was one of the first people the police took down after the Alfano shooting. The police hung the witness out of the window by his ankles at the old police headquarters on 11th and State Streets. As a result, he implicated everybody whom they wanted him to implicate, telling how it went down and everything.
>
> Then, they called him back because he gave some inconsistent information. So, he had told about three stories before I interviewed him. Of course, he said that everything he had previously said was a lie. By the time I finished cross-examining him with all of his different stories, no one took him seriously."

That was the second major obstacle standing in the prosecution's way. Then, by chance, the defense team learned that the prosecution had yet another run at the female witness, who had made the misidentification in court.

Montgomery says:

> A friend of mine, an assistant state's attorney, told us that the prosecution team had tried to intimidate the witness into saying that the defense team had asked her to give false

testimony. Outraged, we told Judge Garippo putting it out in the open and on the record.

In response the judge ordered the prosecutors to approach the bench and, then, admonished them in front of everyone. I would say that those were the main factors that enabled us to gain an acquittal in this very difficult case. That's one case where I had colleagues with whom I enjoyed working.

The legal takeaway from this case? Atty. Montgomery says, *"Don't take any prospective juror for granted."*

THE JACKIE TURNER CASE

In 1969, Jeff Fort and two other Blackstone Rangers were charged with the attempted murder of Jackie Turner, a Vietnam veteran. Atty. Montgomery represented Jeff Fort and the other defendants. He summarizes the case:

There was a veterans group that was organized in Wood-lawn where the Blackstone Rangers operated. There was animosity between the two groups. At some point, Jackie Turner, a member of the veterans group, was walking on 71st Street when a few Blackstone Rangers, including Jeff Fort, allegedly shot him. Jackie Turner did not die. So, the three young men were charged with the attempted murder of Jackie Turner.

We had a jury trial in that case. At the end of the trial, there was a guilty verdict for the three defendants. As a result, we moved to poll the jury. This meant that we would ask the jury, 'Was this and is this now your verdict?' The fourth juror responded, 'It was, but it's not anymore.'

So, we immediately moved for a mistrial. The judge did not know what to do. So, he sent the jury back to deliberate some more. The jurors returned and the case still ended as a mistrial.

Under the circumstances, my clients and I were required to return to court to find out if the case would be retried. I returned to court, but Jeff did not show up. Finally, I reached out to some people to find out what happened. I was informed that he was on his way to court, and the cops were all around. He became afraid that they were going to kill him, and he left.

Later, Jeff was arrested in New York on a warrant for jump-
ing bail in the Jackie Turner case. He was charged with and
indicted as a result of failing to appear in court under the
terms of his bond.

Coincidentally, the Jackie Turner case was pending when he
was indicted—along with other members of the "Main 21"—
in federal court. So, Jeff was never retried on the Jackie
Turner case.

POLICY REVISITED – THE NUMBERS GAME

Policy, or the numbers game, as discussed earlier, began as a way for the black community to both have a little fun, and make a little money when your number hit. It mostly remained our little secret until it grew to the point where both white law enforcement and the Mafia took notice.

Atty. Montgomery says, *"By 1976, the Chicago Mafia had taken over the illegal policy or numbers business operating in the black community. They engaged members of the Nation (P Stone) to oversee the historical black operators on their behalf. This takeover caused the FBI and IRS to begin to police the policy racket. Because I had been representing the leadership of the Nation, I was hired to defend the black policy operatives and the Nation members, when they were indicted by the federal government."*

Time management is one of the issues often confronted by successful criminal defense attorneys. He recalls, *"When the indictment was returned in 1976, I was in the midst of the Black Panther civil trial, involving the murders of Fred Hampton and Mark Clark. I was able to prepare the pretrial motions directed at suppressing the evidence in the policy case, which was essential to obtaining a conviction. I successfully suppressed the evidence and all involved were acquitted. The legal fees I earned in this and other cases enabled me to try the Hampton case, which lasted about eighteen months."*

CONTINUING THROUGH THE 70s

The law practice continued to grow as Atty. Montgomery's name and reputation grew in Chicago's legal circles. As the variety of cases grew, he also consciously began to seek out more personal injury cases, both for the challenges presented and the potential of more money.

He reflects:

In the 1970s, I represented Amtrak and Conrail in several
railroad crossing accidents. The prep work was mostly done
by my partner, the late William Holland, and other associ-

ates. I prepared cases for trial and tried them. I continued to try criminal cases, my passion. Civil defense cases helped with cash flow but yielded little profit—not that criminal cases were much different.

I began to look for personal injury cases where I could generate larger fees. One such case was **Chesney v. Marek**.

This case illustrates how ordinary people can become ensnared in the legal system, when domestic situations spiral out of their control.

Atty. Montgomery picks up the narrative:

Chesney was a young Caucasian man who became enraged after a marital dispute. Following ejection from his in-laws' home where his wife sought refuge, he returned home distraught. The police, whom had been called by his wife to the home, were refused entry when they arrived.

Instead he armed himself with a hunting bow and arrow and pointed it at the police through a closed window. The police responded, firing a shotgun through the window killing Chesney instantly.

At this point, Atty. Montgomery realized that he was still learning how to navigate the various twists and turns of the legal system.

"I tried the case to a successful verdict, but the recovery was low because the jury considered the officers' limited income. The municipality was not sued. This was a lesson learned in unfamiliar territory."

Some of the most interesting legal battles are often the result of some of the most tragic circumstances. Consider the following case. Atty. Montgomery recalls the details:

"I was next retained by a lady who was rendered paralyzed when nurses turned her over to change her sheets. In the process her breathing tube dislodged. Unfortunately, the nursing staff failed to notice the problem. By the time it was discovered and corrected she had suffered neurologic injury, including paraplegia and speech dysfunction. After pretrial and expert discovery, we settled the case for $5.5 million."

BLACK NOTARY FOUND, WHITE MAN STILL MISSING!

Good attorneys advise their clients that it is always in their best interests to tell the truth. Sometimes they listen and sometimes....Well, let's let Atty. Montgomery tell the story.

*During this time, I tried a number of federal criminal cases in Chicago and Indiana. In **U.S. v. Scott**, my client Mr. Scott, had purchased a tractor and trailer from two separate individuals. The trailer was bought in Chicago and the tractor was purchased from a white man in Mississippi. He paid for both on the installment plan and received receipts.*

Turns out, both the tractor and trailer were stolen. Even though when FBI agents interviewed him at his Chicago home, Mr. Scott said he had receipts, including a notarized bill of sale for the tractor. Scott was arrested. My client was later indicted for possession of stolen motor vehicles in interstate commerce.

At trial, I cross-examined the FBI agents and they confirmed that Mr. Scott had produced the notarized bill for the tractor when they interviewed him. I produced the receipts for their review feeling that the case was won.

My client not only had the notarized documents, he claimed that the white man who sold him the tractor had come from Mississippi to deliver the bill of sale. They had then gone to a notary public to complete the deal.

Mr. Scott had promised to produce the female notary so she could testify at trial. I was somewhat concerned that he had been unable to do so. Finally, in mid-trial he told me that he had located her. He described her debilitated condition, making it clear that she could not possibly appear at trial to confirm his story.

I was convinced that Mr. Scott could persuasively tell his story on the witness stand.

Wrong.

After his dramatic and detailed testimony, the case was adjourned until the next morning. When court resumed I announced 'the defense rests.'

I then glanced toward the courtroom door as two FBI agents escorted an elderly, limping black woman toward the witness stand, as a rebuttal witness. As she passed our table she said, 'Morning Mr. Scott.'

As shocked as I was with her appearance and her impending testimony, I remained cool, as if nothing had happened. She, of course, testified that she had notarized the document and that there was no white man with Mr. Scott.

The lady had potentially destroyed my client's credibility and I had no choice but to attempt to discredit her. The problem? I had absolutely no basis upon which to do so. I asked her, 'Mrs. Jones, how old are you?' She fortunately responded, 'I'm seventy-nine, I mean ninety-three.' I triumphantly announced, 'I have no further questions of this witness.'

Mr. Scott was found not guilty. Soon afterward, a male juror called me and asked if I was surprised, when the old lady appeared in the courtroom. I said that I was devastated. He said that I didn't look devastated. He went on to say how incompetent the FBI agents were in failing to look at the receipts when they interviewed Mr. Scott.

Chapter 16
HAROLD!

"I didn't want to be Chicago's Corporation Counsel.
I was finally about to make some money."

Atty. James D. Montgomery, Sr.

Harold Washington's life was an exclamation point! His intelligence, personality, articulation, vision and love for Chicago were phenomenal. He was born to be mayor of Chicago. Many believe that, but for his untimely death in **1987**, he might have served as long as either of the two Daleys.

Richard J. Daley author of big city, municipal bossism, served twenty-one years, from **1955 – 1976**, before his death by heart attack on December 2, 1976.

Michael Bilandic, nurtured and tutored by Richard J. Daley was thrust into office by Daley's still potent machine as a placeholder, having promised not to seek a full term. But he decided, once on the throne, why give it up?

However, the combination of a seven-foot snowstorm and upstart candidate **Jane Byrne**, who ran against him in **1979**, returned him to private practice. Chicagoans slogging around in the snow were convinced that if Richard J. was still in place, the snow would have magically disappeared. Bilandic capped his political career as Chief Justice of the Illinois Supreme Court before passing in 2002 at the age of seventy-eight.

Jane Byrne, also known as the *"forgotten mayor,"* was the first female mayor in Chicago's history. Her election in 1979 is notable because it ended forty-eight years of Democratic Machine rule over Chicago's politics.

Interim Chicago Mayor Michael Bilandic

Chicago Mayor Jane Byrne

Chicago Mayoral Candidate Harold Washington

Chicago Mayor Richard M. Daley

Wielding his unprecedented brand of independent politics, Harold Washington would help maintain the machine's seat on the political sidelines. His coalition of Hispanics, lakefront liberals, and African Americans would usher in a brand of politics never before seen by the city of Chicago.

But, first, he had to win. Confronted by incumbent **Byrne** and **State's Attorney Richard M. Daley**, Washington knew that although a three-way race with two white opponents was an advantage, he still had to raise money and significantly increase the number of black voters.

While he had no desire to be appointed as the city's first black corporation counsel by Chicago's first black mayor, **Atty. Jim Montgomery** had long been involved in the fight to elect a black mayor.

As early as **1974**, he was a leader of the **Committee for a Black Mayor**, as **chair of the search committee**. That year a poll they conducted found that **State Senator Richard Newhouse** had the *"highest name recognition"* of any potential black candidate in the 1976 election. Montgomery was also **president** of the **Cook County Bar Association** at that time. At some point in 1974, **Congressman Ralph Metcalfe** had removed his name from consideration.

Also, in 1974, prominent **Chicago Tribune columnist, Vernon Jarrett** wrote:

"More than 300,000 blacks are believed to be unregistered in Chicago. More than seventy percent don't vote in local elections."

After appealing to wealthy and influential African Americans about the importance of funding and supporting a black candidate, the committee was able to raise about $187,000. But they were both surprised and disappointed about the failure to garner any significant public support from the *"black elite."*

Concerning Metcalfe's withdrawal and lack of overall support, Atty. Montgomery in an interview with Jarrett said:

"One thing we've learned, we must go to the ordinary black citizen and make it known that we want their participation. Dependence on a small group of prominent people won't do the job in a struggle involving our political freedom."

Over the next decade, as the city experienced the death of Richard J. Daley as well as the unspectacular terms of Bilandic, and then Byrne, the independent political movement in Chicago continued searching for a black candidate. But not just any black candidate would do.

They needed an accomplished politician, someone wise to Chicago's unique way of doing politics.

They needed an outsider with insider's skills and access, someone who would be embraced by the monied gentry. They needed someone who could talk the language of the street, someone smart and hip. They needed someone with a sense of humor, someone serious, but centered.

They needed someone who would make the white power structure say DAMN!

They needed Harold Washington.

They wanted him and, ultimately, they got him. But not before more than $250,000 was raised and more than 100,000 black voters were added to the rolls. Many were heroes in this play, but none more so than **Edward Gardner**, then owner of **Soft Sheen Products**. He funded the campaign and spearheaded the massive voter registration effort, *"Come Alive on October 5."* Black-oriented radio was especially important in spreading this message.

In perhaps a prophetic move, **Mr. Gardner,** as he is affectionately known, was also the founder through the **Soft Sheen Foundation**, of the *"Black on Black Love"* program in the 1990s, designed to help stem the then rampant violence in Chicago's black communities. He had been moved to action when a street gang killed a fifteen–month-old baby in 1993.

At that time he said:

"It's time for these young men (gang members) to begin to act like men. Carrying a gun does not make you a man. Assuming the responsibilities of a man by doing the positive things in life are what make you a man."

Black-on-Black Love created several community-based programs including an arts and crafts center in the Robert Taylor Homes and a bank employment-training program, among others.

HAROLD – DESTINED?

Years from now, former Chicago Mayor Richard M. Daley will be remembered for two things: First, his mismanagement of Chicago into near financial ruin and, second, his gift of Harold Washington as Chicago's first black mayor.

Had Daley, then Cook County State's Attorney, dropped out, heeding the wishes of Byrne and others, it is highly unlikely that Washington would have won in a two-person race. Especially in the anti-black racial and political atmosphere of 1983 Chicago.

Honing his independent political skills at **Roosevelt College** (now **Roosevelt University**), where he entered in 1946 at the age of twenty-four and as a war veteran, Washington graduated in 1949 with a Bachelor of Arts degree. Along the way, he was elected third president of the Student Council.

Moving on to Northwestern University School of Law—like James Montgomery, Sr.—he initially was the only black student in his class. He concentrated on his studies, graduating and receiving his law degree in 1952. He passed the bar and began private practice that same year.

THE RACE FOR MAYOR

Washington ran the table in the **February 22, 1983 Democratic primary** with **thirty-seven percent** of the vote. Jane Byrne had thirty-three percent and Daley thirty percent.

In the general election in April, Washington faced a virtually unknown Republican, the historically nondescript Bernie Epton. His racially charged slogan urging people to vote for him, **"Before it's too late,"** attracted huge numbers of voters, including some highly placed Democrats and their ward organizations. Still, Washington managed to win the seat with **51.7%** of the vote.

Perhaps, as an early signal of his divisive intentions, once Harold Washington became mayor of Chicago, Cook County Democratic Chairman Eddie Vrdolyak's ward organization was one of those supporting the Republican Epton.

Of the Chicago mayors before him, no one was better qualified to serve than Harold Washington, the ultimate insider-outsider. Raised on a diet of Chicago Machine politics, Washington repeatedly used his insider's knowledge to weaken the machine and dull its impact on the black community.

LEARNING THE GAME

Congressman Ralph Metcalfe

For all of his deserved reputation as a political independent and reformer, Harold Washington mastered the political game from the inside out. He learned from the **Chicago Democratic Machine**, initially serving as a ward precinct worker, as did his father.

He then worked for **3rd Ward Alderman, Ralph Metcalfe**, his political godfather, after graduating from law school and until he first ran for election to the Illinois House in 1965, with the blessing of Mayor Richard J. Daley. At that time, Metcalfe was an important cog in Daley's South Side political apparatus. Under Metcalfe's leadership, the 3rd Ward was instrumental in Daley's first election in 1955.

It was in the early 1960s that Washington began working with and organizing the 3rd Ward's Young Democratic organization. It was instrumental in helping to organize similar groups in other wards.

158

Conrad Worrill recalls:

> *Black political organizing grew out of the 2nd Ward and flowed into the 3rd Ward. The 3rd Ward Black Political Party Organization was one of the key organizations in black politics in Chicago during that era.*
>
> *So, Harold was kind of a maverick inside the 3rd Ward. He didn't always go along with what they were into. He came up through the Young Democrats. They had a system of procuring jobs and patronage through the ward committeeman. In 1963 there was a dump Daley campaign. In **1967, Dick Gregory** ran as a write-in candidate for mayor. And, in **1971, Rev. Jesse Jackson** announced a run for mayor.*

These activities led to several independent aldermanic candidates winning seats in the late 1960s, setting the stage for Washington's later run for the mayor's seat in 1983, becoming Chicago's first African American mayor. Other groups like the **Chicago League of Negro Voters**, founded in 1958, were also important in this evolutionary process. Washington and **Bennett Johnson**, a well-known journalist and political activist, were among the co-founders. Johnson is also the founder of Path Press, one of the first black-owned publishing houses.

They were constant critics of the Daley Machine and the "Silent Six," including 3rd Ward Alderman Ralph Metcalfe. This organization was also instrumental in the nomination of Atty. Lemuel Bentley to run as City Clerk in 1959 where he received more than 58,000 votes. This was reportedly the first time an African American had run for citywide office. Gus Savage ran Bentley's campaign.

Washington served in the **Illinois House** from **1965–1976**, periodically breaking ranks and supporting independent issues. In 1976, he ran and won a seat in the **Illinois Senate**.

However, as a state legislator in the late 1960s, Washington was ahead of the curve, supporting **Renault Robinson**, who was head and founder of the **African American Patrolman's League**. Robinson gained Washington's support to develop legislation creating a civilian review board to monitor police brutality. This move, which was unsupported by Metcalfe, angered Daley. Fearing Daley, many liberal legislators—black and white—failed to support the effort.

This resulted in Washington first losing and then regaining the party's support for re-election in 1969. He, of course, won re-election. Washington then served from **1976–1980** in the **state senate**.

159

Meanwhile, in **1977**, there was a special mayoral election to choose a successor to Mayor Daley. Washington finished third in a group of four among those running. He then ran and won election to the **U.S. House of Representatives** in **1980**, serving until **1983** when he ran and won the seat to become **mayor** of **Chicago**.

Chapter 17
HAROLD! — CHICAGO'S FIRST BLACK MAYOR

"Washington was a catalyst who brought all the arms
of the movement together."

Former Illinois State Senator Alice Palmer

In an excellent political analysis of Chicago politics from **Daley I** to **Harold Washington, South African Journalist Xolela Mangeu** wrote:

> *Washington knew he needed to build a multi-racial coa-*
> *lition. That was the movement that ultimately swept him*
> *into power, and subsequently provided the basis for his*
> *administration.*
>
> *Harold Washington opened up spaces for individuals and*
> *communities who never would have had a chance to partic-*
> *ipate in government under the political machine.*

What now? Managing a bureaucracy the size and scope of the city of Chicago is a big challenge under the best of circumstances. And the events leading up to Washington's election were anything but ideal.

The old Democratic power structure had already given a preview of what was to come, many of the old guard having bought into Bernie Epton's *"Before it's too late,"* vision of the city by the lake.

Judge Charles E. Freeman of the Cook County Circuit Court inaugurates Mayor Harold Washington, April 29, 1983, Chicago Public Library, Special Collections and Preservation Division, HWAC 1983-04-29: Willy Schmidt, photographer

163

Expectations were high and the obstacles were many.

Once in office one thing was clear, everybody wanted something. Some wanted political empowerment. Some wanted contracts. Some wanted both. Washington and his administration were under tremendous pressure to deliver.

Many supporters believed their lives would change overnight from the Hood to the Gold Coast. Get on board. In truth, some of those who expected the most were the same people who least understood the intricacies and subtleties of big time municipal government.

Few understood the complex hoop dance employed by Vrdolyak and the twenty-nine to keep the mayor from fully wielding the wand of power, mandated by his stunning victory.

The same thing would happen nearly thirty years later on the election of **President Barack Obama**. It was not uncommon for disgruntled *"supporters"* to lambast the newly elected chief executive, on talk radio and other mediums, for not intervening when their lights were cut off.

One of the first tasks was to recruit a top-level executive staff. These were people who had both the skills and political acumen to serve. People like Grayson Mitchell, first press secretary, and William Ware, chief of staff in the first administration. Ware, suffered an untimely death in 1985 at the age of thirty-seven, the victim of pneumonia. He was later replaced by Ernest Barefield.

But, none of this works unless you have the best legal talent. So, one of the first to be contacted was Atty. James Montgomery who reluctantly signed on as Mayor Washington's first corporation counsel. He was the first, and to-date only, African American corporation counsel in Chicago's history.

Reflecting, he says:

"You know Harold was an avid reader. His vocabulary was second to none. It befuddled me from time to time. There were times when I didn't know whether to laugh or look serious. He was also very perceptive in terms of reading people. You'd sit in a meeting with him, and he'd be reading your every move."

As corporation counsel, Jim Montgomery was the mayor's top legal advisor, while also managing a bureaucracy of some one hundred and ninety-five lawyers, including assistant corporation counsels who managed various departments. They all reported to the noted trial attorney. He was accustomed to running his own show, and was anything but a government bureaucrat.

164

Of Mayor Washington he says:

"He was a master politician. I was not."

However, early conflicts revolved more around simple numbers than politics. Chicago's City Council consists of fifty aldermen. The majority bloc headed by Alderman Ed Vrdolyak had twenty-nine votes, including one Hispanic. Mayor Washington's bloc had twenty-one votes.

Until now, those in power had conveniently ignored the fact that Chicago's governmental structure called for a **strong council,**

James D. Montgomery during the Washington Years, 1983

weak mayor. That statutory fact never surfaced during the reign of Richard J. and successors. It was only revived and enforced when the city elected its first black mayor.

Almost immediately, Vrdolyak reorganized the Council placing his backers at the head of the majority of City Council committees. Sixteen of Washington's twenty-one backers were African American. Under the new alignment, they received three chairmanships.

The majority faction, also in rapid order, held Jim Montgomery's corporation council appointment in committee, requiring him to serve in an acting capacity.

Finally, a federal court order initially limited the new administration to hiring only about two hundred and fifty top-level policymaking workers, instead of the twelve hundred they had sought. On appeal, the Washington administration was allowed to hire about eleven hundred and seventy policy makers.

In a Chicago Tribune article, acting Corporation Counsel Montgomery said:

"By this agreement, the mayor is keeping his campaign promise to end the patronage system in Chicago. This agreement will still enable Washington to put into position people who will run an effective government and who are going to change the way city government is run."

Having the right people in the right jobs was especially important because outgoing Mayor Jane Byrne had reportedly hired hundreds of people for key positions on her way out.

Alderman Ed Burke, a top cohort of Vrdolyak's, was the newly appointed **chairman** of the **Finance Committee** under the Council reorganization. And, what might be a surprise to many, he was a longtime friend of Jim Montgomery.

165

"Jim and I were friends long before he became corporation counsel in 1983. We go back to when I was a cop and he was a defense attorney, back in the middle 1960s. After I left the police department, the relationship continued while we were both defense attorneys. He was very active in the Chicago Bar Association's Annual Christmas Spirits Production as a soloist."

Perhaps, only in Chicago politics could you have a situation where two people, Alderman Ed Burke and Dr. Conrad Worrill, who disagreed on most things political, could both respect and be friends with Jim Montgomery.

Alderman Edward M. Burke, 14th Ward

Alderman Burke and Dr. Worrill were, and continue to be, on the opposite ends of Chicago's political spectrum. Burke was a longtime political insider, seeking to maintain power in the wake of the "Movement" that swept Harold Washington into power. Worrill was one of the architects behind the "Movement" and a top advisor to the new mayor. What could they have in common? Jim Montgomery.

Burke states:

"Jim was a great asset to Harold in those days because he could cut across those lines that were so hardened. Because of relationships that he had forged long before he became corporation counsel, people trusted him. They knew that his word was his bond. If he made a commitment, you could take it to the bank."

Worrill explains:

> *Jim might have had the roughest challenge as the corporation counsel that a corporation counsel has ever had because they went to war against Washington. They tried to unseat him. They filed lawsuits. They tried to make it legally impossible for him to sit in the mayor's seat. Then, they reorganized the City Council.*
>
> *Jim Montgomery caught hell every day that he went to City Hall because Vrdolyak, Burke, and that crew were constantly performing disruptive legal maneuvers.*

Atty. Montgomery recalls:

> *My first important challenge was to weed out those staff members who were not performing and those who had outside employment. I hired a deputy from the private sector to create a hiring committee to hire on the basis of merit, and it worked out well.*

In my effort to provide opportunities for African American attorneys to learn to perform lucrative municipal bond deals, I called in the two bond firms we did business with and insisted that they train black co-bond counsel and pay them one third of the fee. After a time, I learned that the firms were doing all the work, doing no training, and paying the co-bond counsels much smaller fees for little or no work. Ultimately I called a meeting with the firms and the co-counsels and laid down the law. Given the large fees involved, no one expressed any overt objections.

Corporation Counsel Montgomery confers with Aldermen (l-r) Vrdolyak and Burke at City Council meeting. Permission granted by Antonio Dickey.

I had to overcome some of the Mayor's white liberal supporters' efforts to undermine me because I did not allow them to interfere in my policy and employment decisions.

Another challenge was trying to convince black contractors to whom we gave opportunities, to perform the contracts independently instead of joint venturing with majority firms. I felt they should enhance their capacity to work independently and grow their businesses.

HAROLD WASHINGTON I

The Players

Among the first brought into the Washington Administration as top advisors were **William Ware** as **Chief of Staff, Grayson Mitchell** as **Press Secretary**, and **James Montgomery** as **Corporation Counsel**. Ware had previously served Congressman Washington as his chief of staff. Mitchell was a respected Chicago-based journalist. Montgomery, probably the best known, was, by then, a top-tier criminal defense attorney.

While all were highly credentialed in their respective fields, they and others in Mayor Washington's first cabinet were criticized by opponents and the media for their lack of political and managerial experience at that level.

Looking back, the real question is where would one get this type of experience, except on the job? These types of power positions were mostly out of reach for black professionals at the time. That's one reason Washington's election was so important and symbolic.

After a thorough review of the books, the mayor discovered that the administration had inherited a $150 million deficit from the Byrne administration. That became the first and most important business, reducing the deficit. Find new revenue. Give power to the people. Not just those who put him in office, but all of the people.

The Opposition

For City Council powerhouses **Eddie Vrdolyak (10th)** and **Ed Burke (14th)**, the mayoral election was more of an intermission than a mandate for change. Determined to maintain their longtime political and economic control, they put their plan in place.

Ed Burke, still alderman of the 14th Ward and Democratic Committeeman, summarizes the conflict as one of power and not racially inspired. In fact, he blames the media for many, of what he believes are, false perceptions:

"Most reporters are lazy and look for ways to portray an issue in simplistic terms. There is nothing simplistic about what happened between 1983 and 1987. It was not about race. It was about power and the ability of many of us who had been in government to continue to be in government, and to continue to advocate for our point of view."

The theatrics of **Council Wars** remain firmly etched in Jim Montgomery's mind. The frustrations, the battles, the ongoing conflicts.

What about **Ed Vrdolyak**?

"He and I were like fire and water during those years. I'll never forget. Harold, one day said to me, after adjourning a meeting where he and Ed had been shaking their fists at each other...Harold said, 'Go talk to him.' I said, I'm not talking to that son of a bitch. He talks to me like I walk on four legs. He said, 'Jim, talk to him.' And (laughing), I did. He was something else."

The Conflicts

From the time he took the oath of office on April 29, 1983 until the court-ordered special elections in May 1986, the Vrdolyak-Burke faction managed to block his every move, voting a solid bloc of twenty-nine votes against whatever the mayor proposed. In any equation, twenty-nine beats twenty-one every time.

Some believed that Washington's strident message at his Swearing-In Ceremony at Navy Pier set the stage for Council Wars. He said in part, *"Business as usual will not be accepted."*

The opposition decided otherwise. Business, as usual, would indeed prevail. Digging in, they opposed the new administration at every opportunity, turning back initiatives, holding up appointments, doing everything possible to make this a one-term disaster.

Even so, with creative use of **Executive Orders**, the Harold Washington Administration managed major accomplishments in the early going.

Triumphs included an improved economy, reduced patronage, open government, citywide economic development. Previously, development had been purposefully limited to mostly the downtown and north side areas.

According to the ***Encyclopedia of Chicago***, the Administration was also able to:

> …cut the city's payroll from an estimated 40,000 down to less than 30,000, erase the city deficit, balance the budget, and broaden freedom of information as public policy. Chicago's bond rating leaped upward, enabling the mayor to push through a $100 million bond issue and the employment of Community Development Block Grants to resurface and repair five miles of city streets in each of the fifty wards.

> He also moved to improve: housing for the poor, after-school and food pantry programs for the homeless, police community relations, equity in Tax Increment Financing (TIF), and city economic planning.

Corporation Counsel Montgomery remembers that early on *"Harold called in all of his top police commanders and said that this (police brutality) must stop. And, it did go down significantly during that time. After his death in 1987, statistics will show that it began to rise again."*

Corporation Counsel Montgomery is credited with:

- **Reforming Corporation Counsel's office**
- **Awarding bond work to black lawyers**
- **Implementing and exceeding thirty percent of city contracts to minorities**
- **Including minorities in major real estate development projects**

Criticized by political opponents who claimed much of this was indeed *'business as usual,'* Corporation Counsel Montgomery responding in a 1985 Chicago Tribune article said, *"Does the city get a dollar's worth for its dollar? I can assure you that in all of the things we have done, we have gotten a dollar's worth for our dollar."*

HAROLD WASHINGTON II

The constant Council battles took their toll on all involved. While the infighting occupied public interest and politicians' time, another battle restoring power to the Washington Administration was about to unfold in federal court.

169

Every ten years following the U.S. Census, ward maps are redrawn reflecting who lives where. Following the Census count in 1980 and during the Byrne Administration in 1981, the Chicago City Council approved new maps. At that time blacks and whites each claimed about forty percent of the city's population, and Hispanics about fifteen percent.

However, the fifty-ward Chicago City Council had thirty-three white aldermen, sixteen black, and one Hispanic. Frustrated over the political gridlock orchestrated by the Vrdolyak bloc of twenty nine aldermen, the Washington forces filed suit in federal court claiming that the existing ward remap unfairly diluted the political power of black and Hispanic voters.

In order to change the equation in the ongoing numbers game between the twenty-nine and twenty-one, the Washington Administration, led by Corporation Counsel Montgomery developed their own empowerment map. It called for the remapping of eight wards into majority Hispanic and black districts.

Conrad Worrill says:

"Jim played a masterful role in helping shape the board's remap fight that led to Harold finally getting enough votes to overturn the twenty-nine and twenty-one. Montgomery was the person who helped legally orchestrate the remap for the wards in the city of Chicago."

After much legal wrangling, including multiple submissions of different maps by both sides, the Washington forces were victorious. In a historic ruling *(Ketchum v. City Council of City of Chicago)* on **Friday, December 27, 1985, U.S District Judge Charles Norgle** approved the redistricting of seven wards, potentially ceding the balance of power to the Washington Administration pending the outcome of the next elections. Those wards were the **22nd, 25th, 26th and 31st (Hispanic)** and the **15th, 37th** and **18th (African American)**.

At the time, Corporation Counsel Montgomery said:

"This map cures the violations of the federal Voting Rights Act (1965) by providing relief to the disenfranchised black and Hispanic voters."

Continuing he said:

"Judge Norgle's ruling provides blacks and Hispanics with the right to elect officials of their choice. We would hope that the remedy to the minority citizenry will be completed by the granting of special elections."
*Source—Chicago Tribune – December 28, 1985

Earlier, prior to the court's decision, Ed Burke had floated a resolution designed to strip Corporation Counsel Montgomery of his authority to represent the entire Council in the remap dispute.

Predictably, following this momentous decision, Vrdolyak announced that despite the court's ruling his side would not just relinquish power. He vowed to recruit a *"strong slate"* to run in the newly remapped wards.

Showing their disdain for Washington, the twenty-nine had retained their own high-priced counsel, saying that the taxpayer authorized and paid corporation counsel did not represent their interests.

In defiance, Montgomery filed a brief in Circuit Court declaring his statutory authority to represent the City Council as a whole body in the matter.

On a historical note, City Council veteran and Vrdolyak stalwart **Vito Marzullo**, the **"Dean of the Council,"** was perhaps the best-known political casualty, as his ward, the 25th, was one of those subject to Judge Norgle's order. Without a ward to represent, he announced his retirement at the age of eighty-eight.

The issue of a special election in advance of the regularly scheduled 1987 election was quickly resolved. In the spring of 1986 special elections were court approved, with Washington backers winning three seats. Still short, **Luis Gutierrez** ran and won in the **26th Ward**, bringing the Council count to **twenty-five and twenty-five** with the mayor able to cast the deciding vote in case of a tie.

Once in control, in rapid order the administration approved:

- **Twenty-five appointments to fourteen boards and departments**
- **Ethics ordinance**
- **Tenant's Bill of Rights**
- **Other pro-consumer legislation**

Mayor Washington at re-election fundraiser organized by the Women's Network, January 25, 1987, Chicago Public Library, Special Collections and Preservation Division, HWAC 1987-01-25: Peter J. Schulz, photographer

Jane Byrne at a Demo-
cratic Unity luncheon,
February 28, 1987,
Chicago Public Library,
Special Collections and
Preservation Division,
HWAC 1987-02-28: Peter
J. Schulz, photographer

Mayor Harold Washington
with Ed Vrdolyak, seated:
Leon Despres July 2, 1985,
Chicago Public Library,
Special Collections and
Preservation Division,
HWAC 1985-07-02: photog-
rapher unknown

Permission granted by Antonio Dickey

172

Chapter 18

PROBLEMS, McCLAIN, RAYMOND – RESIGNATION – RE-ELECTION – DEATH

"Joy and pain are like sunshine and rain."
Frankie Beverly & Maze – R & B Group

The **joy** of winning political office and achieving power and perks are often muted by the **pain** of legal scrutiny by authorities and the persistence of those who—for whatever reason—feel entitled.

This is especially true when the new administration is headed by a black mayor who has vowed, *"Business, as usual, will not be accepted."*

About three years into Washington's first term, in February, 1986, just before the ward remap case was settled, Corporation Counsel Jim Montgomery tendered his resignation. This set tongues a wagging and rumors a flying.

Early on, Montgomery was considered one of the top three or four mayoral advisors. Despite his lack of political experience, his legal acumen, aggressive personality and loyalty to the independent political goals of Mayor Washington were indispensable. So much so that at the point of resignation, Atty. Montgomery was considered Mayor Washington's number one go-to guy in the administration.

He said at the time:

"Almost everything that goes on in the government, at one point or another, I am either involved in or called in to advise the mayor. The mayor has a lot of advisors outside of and inside of the government. I would probably agree that on government matters, it might well be said that I advise him more frequently than other folk. Part of that is the nature of the beast that I am...and the nature of the job as corporation counsel."

*Source—Chicago Tribune - May 26, 1985

Defense Atty. Montgomery in court. Sketch Artist Andy Austin

Further explaining:

"I had planned to stay the full term. But there was a case that I had in Las Vegas, the son of an alleged member of the Mafia, the syndicate; he had been murdered by the police and the case was getting ready to go to trial. I had a partner in Vegas. So, I quit around this time."

The problem is that by then the administration was engulfed in several investigations involving contracts and other alleged internal mischiefs. According to the media and others, the sudden resignation of the chief legal officer demanded further explanation.

Atty. Montgomery states:

*"At that time, a mole named **Michael Raymond** had infiltrated the city government. He was going around (setting up) everyone in government."*

Raymond wasn't just any mole—he was a supreme mole. By the time he was done, he had impacted city government, including several aldermen and administration officials, county government, and the business community.

These events unfolded more than thirty years ago. As usual, when criminal activity occurs and involves multiple players, it is sometimes difficult to determine exactly what happened.

What is clear is that Raymond—found dead of undisclosed causes in an Atlanta jail cell in 1996—played a central role during the Washington administration in sending several public officials to jail. Because of the clandestine nature of his activities, the roles of others remain unclear.

What is known is that in 1985-86, Michael Raymond also known as Michael Burnett—in return for a more lenient sentence after being caught in an attempted robbery in Nashville, Tennessee—agreed to wear a wire for the FBI in order to snare public officials and others in a highly publicized case forever known as **Operation Incubator**.

Raymond also enabled the bureau to capture video footage of various people through a peephole in a Lake Shore Drive apartment in which the agency had set him up.

At the time, the city of Chicago was seeking bids from contractors to oversee collections for overdue parking tickets. This was a multi-million dollar contract attracting the attention of two bidders, **Systematic Recovery** and **Datacom Systems**.

Under the direction of the FBI and acting on behalf of Systematic Recovery, Raymond posed as a corrupt businessman offering bribes to elected and administration officials.

Eventually, the administration, led by top lawyer Montgomery, began investigating. At some point, a sitting federal grand jury was convened, calling Montgomery among others to testify.

Montgomery himself was under fire for not reporting to Mayor Washington and law enforcement authorities a $10,000 payment received by a deputy revenue director from Michael Raymond on behalf of Systematic Recovery.

The deputy revenue director had originally claimed the money was a loan from Clarence McClain, a close friend of the mayor, and former appointee as director of Freedom of Information for the city. He later acknowledged the money was from Raymond and was among those convicted.

As all of this played out in federal court, more than **sixteen** people were convicted, including several Chicago aldermen and city officials. This chilled the Washington Administration that was then re-establishing its political agenda in the wake of the federal remap victory.

Atty. Montgomery was called before a grand jury, but was not indicted after sufficient evidence demonstrated that he did not accept a bribe.

In addition, he had warned the mayor about McClain early on:

"One day I was called into a meeting with Mayor Washington and Ernie Barefield, then chief of staff. Barefield said, 'Jim, the mayor called us together because there is some suggestion that Clarence is interfering in the government.' I said, 'The man is all over the government. Every time I look around, I'm getting a call that he's interfering here, interfering there.' I said the wrong thing. The mayor was not supposed to know that."

This was perhaps a dynamic tension revealing how different the political arena is from the practice of law.

> *I went into government as a non-political person. My total experience with it was throwing stones, suing 'em, and fighting 'em like hell. So, I didn't have any notion about how to behave politically.*
>
> *By the time I learned, I still wasn't always political. When things would come up in staff meetings, I told it like it was. Sometimes bullshit doesn't get you anywhere. You've got to tell the mayor the truth, especially if you're one-on-one. I thought he had to be told. Mayor Washington had already caught a lot of heat behind him in the first place.*

Looking back, **Operation Incubator** was arguably the biggest scandal faced by the Washington Administration. Many within the administration believed that this was mostly a case of the federal government targeting black politicians.

Atty. Montgomery's position is, *"Black officials are prime targets of the government for three basic reasons. First, racism and white supremacy. Secondly, black public officials are sometimes easy targets due to a lack of financial resources and inexperience in the political arena. Third, federal prosecutors make their reputations on high profile political corruption cases, and typically have future higher political ambitions."*

Biggest accomplishments as corporation counsel? *"Preparing an executive order which set goals for minority business participation in city purchases and contracts. Professionalizing the office and getting the respect of the Bench and Bar. Also, empowering minority law firms by farming out legal and municipal bond work. Finally, convincing Mayor Washington not to scuttle the acquisition of the People Mover system at O'Hare Airport."*

However this is viewed historically, scandals have been constant in most political administrations, big and small. Others faced by the Washington Administration include:

The **People Mover Contract** stands out partly because of the importance and magnitude of the project and also because it gave an up close, inside look at power politics.

As corporation counsel, Montgomery was assigned the responsibility of opening the bids. *"I was appointed by the mayor to the task force to investigate the feasibility of acquiring a People Mover system for O'Hare Airport. The group included Public Works engineers, deputy commissioners from the Aviation Department and a few public transportation consultants. They began to look to me for direction given my access to Mayor Washington."*

The work of the task force attracted political, public and media attention early on because: *"We traveled to London, Canada and France to view and inspect other People Mover systems. Our first challenge was to fight media efforts to characterize our trips as boondoggles (at taxpayer expense). Fortunately because of an unforeseen change in our departure time from France, we happily avoided the media reception waiting at O'Hare."*

Continuing he recalls, *"After receiving bids from a French company and Westinghouse, a U.S. company, we analyzed both the long-term and short-term costs of contracting with both companies. The low bid was the French company. However, their long-term costs were much higher."*

Explaining the then corporation counsel notes, *"The French system provided only pairs of cars, while the Westinghouse system only required single cars. In other words, if the traffic requirements only called for one car, the French system would provide two."*

Explaining, the expert engineers reported that based on the concept of *"train ton miles"* –which is defined as a single ton of goods that is transported for one mile—the long-term cost of operating the French system would greatly enhance the cost of long-term maintenance and repair costs.

Montgomery says, *"We announced the selection of Westinghouse and all hell broke loose. Turns out that Vrdolyak was representing the French bids. He rushed to the media suggesting that I had done something improper. There was so much media stink that Mayor Washington, at the suggestion of the task force, rejected both bids as too costly.* He directed each party to consider cost savings that would not compromise the quality of the system."

But that was not the end. In some ways the problems were just beginning. *"Meanwhile, the president of the French company met with me declaring, 'Ziz is not acceptable,' a number of times. I explained the problem and he assured me that he could re-engineer the system to accommodate single cars. Ultimately, the French won the contract and we were sued by Westinghouse. The City of Chicago won the case on the merits after it went to trial because the French had the lower bid."*

But the media was just getting started. Montgomery recalls:

> *They were hot on Harold's trail. He called a cabinet meeting, including members of the task force, seeking opinions as to whether to cancel the award. It was clear that Mayor Washington wanted to quiet the storm. All but one in attendance suggested cancellation. When asked, I forcefully urged the mayor to proceed. I told him that we would win the lawsuit, but meanwhile, his corporation counsel's behind was hanging out the window with people taking potshots.*
>
> *I also said that the project would create jobs, concluding that going ahead was the mayoral thing to do. Harold stood up, angrily terminating the meeting. He said, 'I've taken a lot of heat on this issue.' Later he walked out of his office and said he would like to see me at his apartment on Sunday morning. When I arrived, he said firmly, 'There shall never come a time when you tell me what is mayoral. What I do is mayoral.' I said, yes sir. We had coffee, chatted briefly and I left.*

Continuing he recalled, *"Later, although I was no longer working for the administration, the mayor invited me to the ribbon cutting and opening of the People Mover system."*

MAYOR SECRETLY TAPED IN HIS APARTMENT

Meanwhile, another internal scandal had played out in **January, 1985. James "Skip" Burrell,** a city worker running for 3rd Ward alderman in an eight-candidate special election, was caught and later admitted secretly taping Mayor Washington in a conversation held in the mayor's Hyde Park residence.

In a city long known for outrageous and *"bet you can't top this"* political activity, this prank shot to the top of the list.

During the unauthorized taping, Mayor Washington is heard urging Burrell to drop out of the race.

Former 3rd Ward Alderman
Dorothy Tillman

Also on the tape, Mayor Washington made some questionable, some would say disparaging, remarks about **3rd Ward Alderman Dorothy Tillman**, one of his supporters, and the favorite to retain her 3rd Ward seat. She had been appointed by the mayor to replace then **3rd Ward Alderman Tyrone Kenner** who was forced to resign after a criminal conviction.

This was the reason for the special election. The administration, including Corporation Counsel Montgomery, believed that the intent was to weaken the mayor's political support in the black community. Burrell admitted giving the tape to former Alderman Kenner. The tape later ended up in the Vrdolyak camp.

Despite all of this, Tillman won the seat, remaining 3rd Ward alderman and an active supporter of the Washington administration. She served until her defeat in 2007 by Pat Dowell.

ON TO VEGAS

Montgomery had looked forward to returning to his law practice. He had connected with a Las Vegas attorney and become involved in this case before signing on with the Washington Administration in 1983. Now, in early 1987, the case was going to trial. And Atty. Montgomery was ready to return to work.

In 1980, Frank Bluestein, thirty-five, came to the attention of the Las Vegas Police Department after picking up a pizza at a local restaurant owned by and reportedly frequented by organized crime figures, according to Las Vegas authorities. Atty. Montgomery sheds light on the facts of the case:

> *I went to Las Vegas to plead a case—which I had filed before leaving the Washington Administration as corporation*

counsel—on behalf of a young man who had been murdered by the Las Vegas Police Department. This young man just happened to be the son of a man who was allegedly a member of the Mafia.

So, the son was killed on suspicion that he was a bad guy because he had an Illinois license plate. The Las Vegas police knew he was the son of the alleged Mafia guy, and they trailed him from a Mafia pizza place back to his house. It scared the man and he ended up trying to shake the police once he realized that they were following him.

The young man stopped before he went to his house where his wife was. He stopped in the driveway. Then, the police pulled up behind him, and he points a gun out of his car window believing these men to be criminals. Keep in mind that he had been run off the road maybe two or three weeks before. So, the young man's brother had said, 'Here, take this gun and keep that with you.' So, when the young man pointed the gun that his brother had given him the police blew him away.

Of course, the man didn't know that the people following him were police. It was an unmarked car. He didn't know who the hell it was. It could have been a killer.

The undercover police had on dirty clothes, regular jackets. They had Arizona license plates on a sports car. So, the young man did not think they were police.

So, I went and finished trying that case and, unfortunately, rejected an $800,000 offer and ended up getting a Mormon jury. The case went down the drain because most of my witnesses were Mafia guys who had gone to the hospital after he had been shot, all that evidence came in and, of course, they were notorious characters.

In court, testimony revealed that the policemen were interested in him because of his Illinois plates. It turns out that Bluestein had just recently moved from the Chicago area. That might explain the plates.

As Chicagoans know all too well, these stories often ended badly, as it did in this case. Following Bluestein in an unmarked car with Arizona plates, the plainclothes detectives explained, that they fired nineteen times at Bluestein, hitting him four times in the back, as he sat in the front seat of his car. Claiming they believed he might have mob connections, they said he pulled a gun on them.

181

The lawsuit, filed on behalf of his parents Steve and Rose Bluestein, originally sought $22 million in damages, later dropped to $1.6 million. Atty. Montgomery and his Las Vegas partner handled the case on a percentage basis. He had originally hoped to collect a $1 million fee.

In court, Montgomery used a tactic that he had used on at least one other occasion, interviewing an empty chair. The chair represented witnesses that the officers' defense refused to call, whom Atty. Montgomery felt were essential to the case.

Published reports about the case also reveal Montgomery at his dramatic best, raising and lowering his voice "to a whisper" for effect. Numerous bible references, and pausing to mop his brow, were also used to impact the jury. He accused the two police officers of lying on the witness stand.

"Frankie Bluestein was a hardworking, six-day-a-week guy on his day off. He hadn't spat on the street. He hadn't done anything wrong. They didn't know if he was a priest or a pimp. They didn't know who he was."

But all to no avail. The jury dismissed all charges, sending the two undercover officers back to the streets in their unmarked car, with out-of-state plates.

Making matters worse, Atty. Montgomery and his colleague had earlier rejected an offer of an $800,000 annuity, which would have eventually paid $4 million. Instead, they rolled the dice and lost…Nothing to show for four months in Vegas, countless hours of research and preparation, eight weeks of grueling trial work.

At trial's end, he said, *"I was shocked at the outcome. The Bluestein family took the verdict very well."*

Welcome back!

After being a major player in the Washington administration, Atty. Montgomery handled a variety of cases. *"My practice changed dramatically. I began to lobby for health maintenance organizations (HMOs) at the City, Park District and Board of Education. This was lucrative. I was also hired by the City Colleges system to assist in labor negotiations, but that was short-lived."*

Sometimes there is a dynamic tension between one's integrity and the unwritten requirements of the job. In this case, *"A member of the bargaining team got me fired. I was considered a competitive threat because I refused to sit silently and get paid while they ran the negotiations. I was not about to be complicit in such dishonest activity. I would not have respected myself."*

"I began to accept cases from the Chicago Transit Authority and the State's Attorney General's office. I also took on the occasional substantial personal injury case. Much of the defense work was done by my associates. My involvement was limited to preparing and conducting cases that went to trial."

1987 — HAROLD RE-ELECTED

Mayor Harold Washington being sworn in by Judge Charles E. Freeman for his second term, May 4, 1987, Chicago Public Library, Special Collections and Preservation Division, HWAC 1987-05-04: photographer unknown

With Washington's 1983 win in the three-way race between him, Jane Byrne, and Richard M. Daley fresh in mind, Mayor Washington's opposition tried another tactic.

With Ed Vrdolyak and Thomas Hynes, Cook County Assessor, running as independents, Washington won the primary with **fifty-four percent**, including almost **one hundred percent** of the **black vote**.

In the general, Washington again hit **fifty-four percent**, with Hynes withdrawing just before Election Day.

He was just settling in for what he expected to be a relatively peaceful second term when....

HAROLD HARD AT WORK AND THEN...

Hard at work in his fifth-floor office with Press Secretary Alton Miller, Harold Washington collapsed and died of a massive heart attack. Multiple attempts to revive him...in the office...en route to Northwestern Memorial Hospital failed.

Wednesday, November 25, 1987, the day before Thanksgiving.

Mayor Washington had begun that day like many, working on behalf of the city he so loved. This time, he was officiating at a low-income housing groundbreaking ceremony at 46th and Woodlawn. Several city officials, including his

183

City Council Floor Director Alderman Tim Evans (4th) were present.

Everything seemed okay. The Mayor was the same high-spirited Harold, rejuvenated by his recent re-election. He now often boasted that he would be mayor for twenty years.

It turned out he was mayor for life, his life.

He had been warned that he was overweight, two hundred eighty-four pounds at the time of death. The mayor also had the usual maladies—high blood pressure and hypertension—suffered by black men. He was known for not taking care of himself as well as working too hard, and eating all of the wrong foods.

Even so, conspiracy theories swirled. He had been poisoned. His political enemies were responsible. His personal doctor, **Dr. Antonio Senat**, tried to stem the rumors, confirming no foul play was involved. **Cook County Medical Examiner Robert J. Stein** reported that the only drug in the mayor's system was **lidocaine**, a heart stabilization medication, used after a heart attack.

Former Interim Mayor David Orr, later Cook County Clerk

The political shenanigans to determine Mayor Washington's successor didn't help to calm things down. Instead, passions were inflamed. **Alderman Tim Evans**, later **Chief Judge of the Cook County Circuit Court**, and his backers were claiming succession rights, based on the fact that he had been the mayor's handpicked Council floor leader. Others thought differently.

Meanwhile, **Alderman David Orr**, later Cook County Clerk, took office as interim mayor based on his statutory position as the vice-mayor.

GOODBYE HAROLD

The city mourned. The politicians fought. The activists fought. Chicago was once again in turmoil—a familiar place.

On **Monday, November 30, 1987, Mayor Harold Washington** was eulogized in a service at **Christ Universal Temple**, presided over by his **pastor, B. Herbert Martin**. He lies overseeing his city at **Oak Woods Cemetery** on **Chicago's South Side**. The cemetery is one of many in the city that is famous as a resting place for people of prominence. It is also infamous for once having refused to inter people of color.

184

Days earlier, more than **one half million mourners** flowed past his casket to get one last look at **Harold**, the "People's Mayor."

Atty. Montgomery articulates the significance of Mayor Washington's death:

> *For the first time in Chicago's history we had a mayor who believed in providing public service to the whole community and not just to those who had clout.*

> *Prior to Mayor Washington's death, he had finally reached a point where the white community had accepted him as their mayor. This was a guy who would have been mayor for as long as he would have wanted to be mayor of Chicago, because there were even white people who had not gotten public services that got them while Harold was mayor.*

> *Also, what I saw after the debacle between Sawyer and Evans was the end of any realistic opportunity in the near future to get another black mayor elected. Immediately after Harold Washington was elected, they changed the rules so that you'd never have two whites running against one black again.*

> *You also have business going right back to the way it was before, except that the Shakman Decrees had forever gotten rid of political hiring.*

> *Harold was a progressive mayor. He was an unselfish mayor. He didn't want anything for himself. He wasn't out there to get rich. He had never been rich, and did not try to get rich.*

> *He was also a guy who felt like he was not going to just make a few people rich. What he did was for the entire community. So, I think that's a big loss for us.*

> *It's a big loss for the black community because during the whole time he was mayor, police brutality went down dramatically. Of course, it went back up as soon as he left.*

> *For me, you miss a guy who was really a lot of fun. He was an extremely brilliant person who was really a challenge to engage because he was such a prolific speaker and he had such a prolific vocabulary. So, sometimes you did not know what he was saying. He was not being pompous about it. He was a voracious reader.*

THE AFTERMATH

What happened next is among the most despicable chapters in the history of the city of Chicago. The political factions emerged once again. The "progressive" group, including some of Mayor Washington's most ardent supporters, claimed Tim Evans as the obvious choice to become acting mayor.

The other group, including some of Vrdolyak's supporters, claimed Alderman Eugene Sawyer (6th), the quieter of the two aldermen. Some mistook his quiet demeanor and the fact that he was better liked by Vrdolyak's group to mean that he was against the progressives.

Acting Mayor Eugene Sawyer, also Former 6th Ward Alderman

The fact is both were Democratic veterans. They just had different personalities. The black community probably could have lived with either, at least short term. However, it wasn't that simple.

As it turned out, people hit the streets. City Hall was surrounded. Friend turned against friend. Many denounced Sawyer as an "Uncle Tom." In an angry moment, for some reason during a meeting, Alderman Dick Mell jumped on his desk, adding to the general disorder.

When the disorder calmed enough for the City Council to take a vote, **Sawyer** won with **twenty-nine votes** to **nineteen** for **Evans**. As acting mayor, Sawyer was successful in passing some legislation first initiated under Washington, most notably Chicago's first **Human Rights Ordinance in 1988.**

Disorder resumed.

Atty. Montgomery describes what accounts for the tragedy of black electoral politics:

"More often than not, aspirants to public office do not consider what is in the best interests of the black community. The competition between Aldermen Sawyer and Evans is a classic example."

POSTSCRIPT

For all intents and purposes, Chicago's independent political movement died with Harold Washington. Acting Mayor Sawyer ran for a full term in the Democratic primary in 1989. He, and three others, were defeated by Richard M. Daley who went on to win the general election. Daley served until he chose not to run in 2011.

Mayor Washington's political operation—the **Political Education Project (PEP)**—also closed down when the mayor passed. Formed in 1984 after his 1983 election, PEP raised funds, supported candidates, recruited volunteers, and did other activities enabling Washington to extend his political reach.

Friends and colleagues who worked with him knew that his **legacy goal** was to establish **Chicago** as a **national model** for **progressive, independent politics**.

Since his death, Chicago has had difficulty mounting a credible African American mayoral candidate. The black political community remains disconnected since the mayor's death. Some of the animosity developed in the immediate aftermath of Harold's death remains.

James Montgomery reflects, *"Part of the problem is the overall failure of the black community to participate in the electoral process. Harold was a unique candidate. He was well known in the community. He was charismatic and the community trusted him as a politician who would historically veer from the party line and foster the interests of the black community."*

Continuing, *"Some wards in the black community would regularly have turnouts of twenty to thirty percent. We have been unable to develop a process whereby the community selects the candidate. Individuals present themselves and exercise their right to run for public office. We then "split" the vote and all black candidates lose."*

Warming to the subject he notes, *"Recent attempts to call together business and community leaders in an ongoing effort to develop and support viable black candidates have failed. The independence of the group has been compromised by individuals accepting positions in the current administration, while claiming to remain a part of the group whose purpose is in direct conflict with the administration."*

He offers a historical analysis, explaining why the black community continues this behavior. *"Unfortunately, personal ambition often trumps concerns for the common good. This reflects the continuity of the divisiveness visited on our ancestors while chattel slaves. The slave mentality is unfortunately (even if inadvertently) maintained from generation to generation. Much of it is on "us", and much of it is perpetrated by the powers that be who educate us, and who expose us to subtle media brainwashing."*

Chapter 19

BACK TO BASICS

"Where do we go from here?"

Dr. Martin Luther King, Jr.

Crafting a new game plan after the adrenalin pumping, thump-thump-thump of the Washington administration was challenging. But, the now fifty-four-year-old attorney needed new challenges. He also needed money.

As Corporation Counsel and a central character in the Washington drama, Montgomery had maintained a high-profile and name recognition. Now, he needed to reignite his law practice.

While Corporation Counsel, Montgomery says, *"The law firm was in the capable hands of my son so it was easy to transition back to my practice."*

The family now had six children and there was college and all of the other basic expenses to take care of.

As a top-tier defense attorney with a long history of successes, many of which received heavy media attention, Atty. Montgomery didn't have to wait long.

On Wednesday, April 6, 1988, **Howard Medley**, longtime businessman on Chicago's South Side, and contributor to African American causes, was hit with a federal grand jury indictment.

The charge? That Medley, a **Chicago Transit Authority board member**, had accepted $25,000 from a representative of a company holding a CTA contract. Medley admitted to the payment, calling it a finder's fee for a commercial property that he had helped lease.

Medley, who was sixty-one years old at the time, was best known for **Medley Movers**, the far South Side company that he started in 1964. Previously he was a trustee of the **Chicago Board of Elections**, and well known in political and civic circles.

Atty. James Montgomery was hired by Medley, later joined by Atty. Ed Genson.

Brian Flisk, owner and chairman of **Metropolitan Petroleum Company**, which had won a **$38 million** contract with **CTA** to provide diesel fuel, in

Defense Attorney Montgomery addresses jury, Sketch Artist Marcia Danits

Defense Attorney Montgomery in court, Sketch Artist Marcia Danits

1986 and **1987**, was also indicted. The contract included a clause giving the agency deep discounts for on-time payment of invoices.

Metropolitan reportedly believed that the agency would not pay on time, resulting in additional profits for the company. So, imagine their surprise when CTA did indeed pay on time.

Eventually, Metropolitan began purposefully sending late statements, including some false invoices, forcing late payments by CTA. There were also questions about the quality of some of Metropolitan's fuel shipments.

Once this pattern was noticed, an internal investigation was launched. Board Member Medley was suspected of interfering with the investigation by intervening with several staff members, and at least one board member. According to prosecutors, the $25,000 payment was in return for his efforts to end the probe.

Metropolitan's contract also called for inclusion of a minority subcontractor, per Chicago's minority set-a-side requirements, first enacted during the Washington administration. There were serious questions about whether the minority fuel supplier listed by Metropolitan, was providing services, or was a **sham contractor**.

Called and questioned by Atty. Montgomery, **CTA's Superintendent of Investigations**, **Charles Glass**, testified that after Medley had asked him to investigate the contractor, he determined that he was an African American and that he did have enough trucks to fulfill his capacity as a subcontractor.

During and since that time, sham contractors have often been used to avoid both the letter and spirit of city, county, state and federal set-a-side requirements.

Eight people, including Medley, were indicted on various charges. Citing a motion from Atty. Montgomery, Trial Judge **Charles Kocoras**, later granted Medley a separate trial, ruling that some of the charges did not apply to him. Several defendants eventually pleaded guilty, agreeing to cooperate with the government.

Just before going to trial in November, 1988, **conspiracy** and **extortion** charges were dropped against Medley. An agitated Judge Charles Kocoras took time to berate federal prosecutors for what he termed, *"grand jury abuse."*

Medley remained accused of **bribery** and **perjury**. Prosecutors maintained that he had lied about the $25,000 payment when testifying before the grand jury.

Entrapment is the defense often employed by attorneys in these types of cases. Yes, my client took the money, but he would not have been inclined to do so but for the evil influence of the government. That's how it often goes.

There was no question in this case that the money was offered and received. The accused didn't deny it. His attorneys didn't deny it. If not entrapment, what happened? Why did Howard Medley accept $25,000 from a company doing business with an agency on whose board he sat?

"Howard Medley is a giver, not a taker," said Montgomery. *"They (prosecutors) talk very little about the evidence. The evidence will show that this prosecution is ill-conceived. It is smoke without fire."*

Atty. Montgomery continued saying, *"Flisk did not give Medley $25,000. Medley earned the $25,000 from Robert Sperling and Michael Zavis, who were partners in a real estate deal (also lawyers)."*
*Source – Chicago Tribune November 9, 1988

This is where it gets somewhat complicated.

At some point, Sperling, who was previously a Medley acquaintance, inquired whether Medley might be interested in moving Medley Movers into a recently vacated commercial property. Medley wasn't interested, but reportedly indicated that he would look out for a buyer. In return, Sperling promised a substantial finder's fee.

Sometime later Flisk, while meeting with Medley, mentioned that he was looking for a larger building to house Metropolitan. *"So Howard Medley put Flisk and Sperling together and thought no more about it,"* Montgomery said.
*Source – Chicago Tribune, November 9, 1988

Eventually, it was realized that the $25,000 would either have to be considered a real estate commission or a finder's fee. The law prohibits people who don't have real estate licenses from accepting or splitting proceeds from the sale or lease of real estate.

Enter **John Wilson**, whose accounting firm included Medley's accountant. He testified that he contacted an attorney to determine if the $25,000 could be legally characterized as a finder's fee, given the factual circumstances. That attorney, according to his testimony, never got back to him. The property was later leased, not sold.

Meanwhile, Wilson, who was still under oath, testified that in **April, 1987**, one of Flisk's business partners gave him a $25,000 check. He deducted $2,500 as his fee, later giving the remaining $22,500 to Medley. In **July, 1987**, the **CTA Board** terminated the Metropolitan contract for **fraud**.

In **November, 1988**, a few days before the case went to the jury, prosecutors dropped three of the four perjury counts against Howard Medley. Remaining was one perjury count and one bribery count.

192

CLOSING ARGUMENTS

In what was described by **Chicago Tribune reporters John Gorman and Gary Washburn** *"as an emotional ninety-minute argument,"* Atty. Montgomery characterized most of the witness testimony against his client as having been cobbled together by the prosecution shortly before the trial began, and not presented before the grand jury that indicted Medley.

"I'm not suggesting to you anything less than witness tampering."

Most, but not all, of the jury heard Montgomery's plea. On **December 2, 1988**, the trial resulted in a hung jury with eleven–one for acquittal on the perjury charge; and eight–four for acquittal on the bribery charge. Unanimous verdicts are required for acquittal.

POSTSCRIPT

Attys. Montgomery and Genson later withdrew in a dispute over more than $100,000 in legal fees.

Medley said, *"I wanted to pay for the job to be done, and that job hasn't been done yet."*
*Source – Chicago Tribune

He did ultimately agree to pay the lawyers' fees.

He was also reportedly concerned that his attorneys refused to allow him to take the stand to testify in his own defense. Although this reluctance by criminal defense attorneys is common, in the final analysis, it is the client's call. Medley could have chosen to act against his attorneys' advice.

In quick order, Howard Medley selected **Atty. Stanley Hill** as his new lead attorney. The retrial resulted in Medley's conviction.

On appeal to the **United States Court of Appeals, Seventh Circuit**, Medley was represented by **Atty. George Leighton**, who later became the first black Illinois Appellate Court Justice. That appeal was lost as well.

Judge Leighton capped his career as a U.S. District Court Judge and celebrated his 105th birthday on October 22, 2017. The Leighton Criminal Court Building was named in his honor. He was a mentor to a countless number of attorneys, including Atty. Montgomery.

Atty. Montgomery offers additional insight, *"After Medley's conviction and unsuccessful appeals, he served his sentence. He was very embarrassed by his criminal record. He had no sense of moral wrongdoing and felt his conviction was a miscarriage of justice. I agreed."*

Continuing, *"He felt that I was most familiar with his case history, and asked me to file a post-conviction proceeding attacking the conviction collaterally. He then paid the balance of my fee. We were able to develop a factual basis for establishing the unfairness of his trial, and uncover evidence of innocence not presented at his trial. Unfortunately, the court refused to consider the merits of our claims."*

Over the years, the name **Howard Medley** has infrequently surfaced. He remains a contributor to African American causes. As recently as late **2016**, he contributed several trucks to the **Rainbow PUSH Coalition's** humanitarian mission to flood-ravaged **Baton Rouge, Louisiana**. The trucks carried donated food, clothes, sanitary items and water to thousands of residents in the area.

NEXT UP – HARVEY, ILLINOIS

Roughly twenty-five miles and thirty minutes from downtown Chicago via I-57, Halsted or Sibley Boulevard/Western Avenue, lies **Harvey, Illinois**, one of the best known, most- maligned suburbs south of Chicago.

Harvey, not necessarily where you would expect to find a top lawyer like Jim Montgomery practicing his craft. But like doctors and gunslingers, lawyers go where there is work to be done.

And, in **1988** there was work to be done in Harvey.

Harvey is probably best known as the home of **The Dells**, stellar rhythm and blues artists. Others may also recall that the long-shuttered **Dixie Square Mall** was the site of the car chase scene in the ***"Blues Brothers,"*** starring the late **John Belushi** and **Danny Ackroyd**.

It is also known for the long tenure of former **Mayor David N. Johnson, 1983 – 1995**, the city's **first African American mayor**. It is Mayor Johnson who offered Atty. Montgomery the position of Corporation Counsel in 1988.

Former Harvey Mayor David N. Johnson and Atty. Montgomery

He says, *"I was familiar with Atty. Montgomery and the great work he had done on behalf of Mayor Harold Washington. My previous Corporation Counsel, Leo Holt, recommended him to me. They were friends and outstanding attorneys. Both were progressive and strongly identified with the Civil Rights Movement. They projected the image of strong African American men who understood our history of struggle in the United States."*

194

There was also another important reason for bringing in the Montgomery Firm, Johnson recalls:

"I was involved in our version of 'Council Wars.' I believed that Jim fit the bill perfectly and would not be rattled by political events in the Harvey City Council. Plus, James Montgomery had tremendous stature. I hoped that we would benefit from being associated with his firm. I also felt I could learn a lot from him because of his many years of experience."

Remember, Atty. Montgomery at first did not want the corporation counsel position in the Washington administration, feeling he wasn't political enough and the pay didn't compare to what he was used to making.

Now, he found himself thrust into another municipal melee. In a way, history was somewhat repeating itself. Mayor Johnson was another first time black mayor seeking to implement political reforms, fighting politicians determined to have their way.

Putting things into perspective, the former mayor says:

"I had a mindless bloc of commissioners who opposed virtually everything I put forth, just because it was coming from my side of the house. At that time, Harvey operated under the Commission form of government, allowing any three commissioners to arrange city government as they saw fit. There was great overlapping, duplication, and inefficiency in the way city government functioned."

Continuing he noted:

"For example, the Street Department, Water Department and Police Department purchased gasoline from three different companies. This was both inefficient and costly. We weren't monitoring the use of gasoline and other supplies. When I called for the elimination of these practices, the commissioners more or less declared war on me."

Explaining further, former Mayor Johnson said:

"Commissioners who served as administrators (liaisons) of individual departments used their legislative powers to enhance their departments, and at the same time, castrate me as the mayor. This was at the heart of Harvey's Council Wars and their (later) opposition to Jim Montgomery."

Once on board, there was plenty of work for the new corporation counsel and his staff to do. High on the list of problems was a longtime practice of discriminatory hiring practices, pay, job descriptions and vacation time.

"We found secretaries in various departments doing essentially the same work at different levels of pay and benefits. What they made depended on their subjective relationships with the commissioner in charge. One can imagine the amount of exposure to discrimination suits we found when I (first) took office."

195

Johnson continues:

> *Historically, African Americans lived on the West Side*
> *of the city. So, historically speaking, municipal service*
> *delivery began on the East Side of the community where the*
> *white community lived. The majority of city employees also*
> *lived on the East Side.*
>
> *This was the legal climate that Jim's law firm was asked to*
> *address, in a highly-charged political atmosphere. I was*
> *delighted to have him to help me address the economic*
> *crisis in Harvey created by de-industrialization and global-*
> *ization, created by longtime discrimination and legislation*
> *passed like NAFTA.*

Integrity and **honesty** are two concepts that are often missing in political relationships. Over the course of working with Atty. Montgomery, Mayor Johnson realized that he had the necessary legal skills and that his word could be trusted.

> *When I first hired **James Montgomery & Associates**, he*
> *agreed that if I lost control of the Council, he would not*
> *serve as attorney for my opponents. This had happened to*
> *me before, and I had the misfortune of having an attorney*
> *I had hired work for my City Council opponents. They*
> *proceeded to dismantle the initiatives I had begun in order*
> *to overcome discrimination in the operation of Harvey's*
> *government.*
>
> *This left a terrible taste in my mouth. Jim and I discussed*
> *this and he agreed that he would resign if this happened.*
> *The fact that he kept his word, and stepped down after the*
> *balance of power shifted in the City Council, is a glowing*
> *testament to his character and integrity. He walked away*
> *from a minimum of $500,000 of billings. Because of this*
> *and his consummate legal skills, I will always hold James*
> *Montgomery in the highest regard!*

Mayor Johnson also credits the Montgomery Firm, and especially the efforts of **Associate Jean Templeton**, the firm's point person for Harvey, with restoring him to the ballot when he sought to run for a third term in 1991.

An oversight in filling out his economic interest statement caused Johnson to be challenged and initially removed from the ballot. At the time he had been a professor at South Suburban College for more than fifteen years, a well-known fact. Nevertheless, he mistakenly answered no to the question asking whether he had worked for any other governmental units in the past year.

196

Thanks to Atty. Templeton's legal efforts, Johnson won the right to remain on the ballot when the case was tried in **Cook County Circuit Court**. However, the lower court ruling was overturned on appeal. Johnson won and was restored to the ballot, after appealing to the **Illinois Supreme Court** in *Welch v. Johnson*. This set the stage for him running and winning his third consecutive term, serving until **1995**.

A discrimination suit that was later filed and won by Atty. Montgomery against the **Chicago Area Transit Study** (**CATS**) helped to enhance the city of Harvey economically. Because of its location, Harvey remains a major transit hub. **CATS** was the six-county metropolitan transit agency that disbursed transportation funding to municipalities in metropolitan Chicago.

Johnson says:

*"Harvey sued **CATS** after submitting eleven grant applications which were all denied. We realized that this action was part of a pattern of discrimination by **CATS** against the south suburban region in general, and Harvey in particular."*

Continuing he recalls:

*"Because of our suit and I believe the reputation of James Montgomery and his firm, we won. The next year the city was the top recipient of funds from **CATS** and the **Illinois Department of Transportation**."*

More than twenty years later, Mayor Johnson has retired from South Suburban College and electoral politics. He remains active as a consultant, speaker, and advocate for the African American community.

Of Atty. James Montgomery, he says:

"Today, James Montgomery stands at the top tier of Chicago attorneys. He ranks high on my list because he has always identified with the aspirations of the African American community, justice, and equality. A man from humble origins, he has never lost sight of where he came from. I feel privileged to have worked with him and to have received valuable counsel from him and other legal minds like the late Honorable R. Eugene Pincham."

Chapter 20

OPERATION SILVER SHOVEL — ANATOMY OF A DEFENSE

"Minority groups predicate their survival on strategy.
Majority groups on strength."

Gordon Blaine Hancock – Minister - Sociologist

The Montgomery Firm continued to thrive **post Harold Washington**, taking on an interesting array of cases.

While the **Medley trial** and multi-year stint as **Harvey's Corporation Counsel** occupied major portions of **Atty. Montgomery's** intellectual time, increasing numbers of defendants found themselves checking on the attorney's interest and availability to help them solve their various legal dilemmas.

THE DEFENSE NEVER RESTS

Just like sports fans are not interested in watching athletes prepare for the game, those interested in the legal process only want to see the finished product played out in court. Few are ever exposed to the thinking, legal analysis, sifting of evidence and other details that go into the preparation of a client's defense.

Operation Silver Shovel, which hit the Chicago courts in the late 1990s had all the elements of great legal fiction, except it was true. The stars? Corruption, greed and enticement, better known in legal terms as ENTRAPMENT.

In a presentation at the annual meeting of the **International Academy of Trial Lawyers** on **May 22, 1998**, at the Four Seasons Hotel in Chicago, Atty. James Montgomery offered a rare, inside look at legal strategy used to combat entrapment.

OPERATION SILVER SHOVEL

    I.   Structure of Investigation or Sting

        A. Use of Corrupt Cooperating Individuals

            1. Public Official Caught in Corruption

            2. Corrupt Contractor

Attorney James D. Montgomery, Sr., Sketch Artist Andy Austin

B. The corrupt public official or cooperating individual (CI) is used to either introduce undercover agents (UCA) to other police officers, or to make recorded corrupt proposals to public official.

C. The use of video and tape recordings to record meetings, telephone calls and exchanges of money. Also use of video to record the tendering of United States currency to public official.

D. There is an investigative team of prosecutors and federal agents, IRS or FBI, who direct the undercover investigation.

   1. They receive reports of corrupt meetings and conversations and give direction to the undercover agents and confidential informant as to what steps to take next.

   2. The team is directed at two principal objectives. (a)Targeting an official to whom corrupt proposals are to be made, and (b) Developing and implementing phony and real scenarios to induce the targeted official to accept United States currency in exchange for official action.

II. The legal framework guiding the sting investigation

A. Extortion, racketeering, conspiracy, failure to report bribe income and mail fraud are the offenses, which typically flow from these sting operations.

B. The investigative teams use the legal parameters of these statutory offenses to structure the sting operation.

200

III. The scenario created in Chicago's Operation Silver Shovel

    A. A corrupt trucking and recycling contractor was caught in a major bank fraud and induced to cooperate with the feds. He had a reputation as a Mafia-connected individual, and typically bribed city inspectors, aldermen, and other public officials to avoid environmental violations and to get trucking contracts and concrete recycling sites.

    B. The Sting Team initially had the CI, John Christopher, to corrupt a city alderman.

    C. The CI put the city alderman on the payroll at $900 a month under the guise of payments to introduce the confidential informant to "corrupt" aldermen or suburban mayors to: (1) Get recycling sites in their wards or towns, or (2) To get them to use city sanitation resources to assist the CI with cleaning up his work sites.

    D. Not the greatest defense because it rarely works. The client must first be guilty of the charges and usually will have confessed to the crimes "in the language of the Extortion Statutes."

IV. Defense Strategies

    A. Comb through all tape and video recordings thoroughly.

    B. Look for evidence of seduction of the client by the UCA and/or CI – From buying of lunch and cocktails – boasting of large sums of money – the display of large wads of cash – promises of long- term corrupt relationship.

    C. Look for evidence of reluctance to engage in corrupt activity by the client – From refusal to accept money at first, to statements indicating no previous corrupt behavior or efforts to avoid taking money.

    D. Look for recorded strategies between the CI and UCA to induce the targeted public official to take money.

    E. Look for evidence that the client has an exemplary record as a public official with no stains on his record.

    F. Get judge to give entrapment instructions.

The Trial

Admit to jury from opening statement to closing that your client will admit that he took the money, but was induced by government agents to do so.

Sell Them – That, but for the government's seduction:

- **Client would not be a criminal**

- **Contrast the client's prior sterling reputation and character as law-abiding with the criminal, corrupt background of the Cooperating Individual**

- **Keep the jury focused on the fact that the transactions were created (initiated) by the government**

THE TRIAL OF JOHN BOLDEN

Life is complicated. People often are not quite whom or what they seem. It pays to be careful what you say…Whom you say it to…And, how you say it.

Especially if you are a public official.

This would have been good advice in 1997 for former **Chicago Water Commissioner, John Bolden**, when he reportedly promised to put a trucking company *"right at the top of the list,"* for work with the city's Water Commission.

The problem? As Bolden would later discover, the "trucking company honcho" was an undercover FBI agent wearing a hidden wire.

Permission granted by Chicago Sun-Times

Perhaps Bolden would have been more alert if a city alderman—who reportedly received monthly payoffs in return for personal introductions—had not warmly introduced the undercover operative to him. That alderman, later pleaded guilty, in what infamously became known as **"Operation Silver Shovel."**

This was but the latest in a series of public corruption scandals that had rocked Chicago, including **Operation Greylord (1983) and Operation Incubator (1986)**.

Enter **Atty. James Montgomery** who immediately realized that Bolden had been entrapped by the feds. **Atty. Thomas Marzewski** served as co-counsel.

202

Legally, **entrapment** is a sustainable defense when it is proved that the defendant would not have committed the act, but for the actions and enticement of the prosecution, in this case representing the federal government.

At trial in **Judge Blanche Manning's** courtroom, the alderman, who had already pled guilty admitted that he:

- **Did not know Bolden well**
- **Did not know Bolden to be corrupt**
- **Lied because he wanted to continue receiving payoffs**

In his own defense, Bolden testified that he:

- **Got involved to avoid offending the alderman**
- **Was surprised at the payoff offer – twice**
- **Wanted to return the money**
- **Admitted that the alderman warned him that a bribe would be offered**

Bolden also admitted that when first confronted by FBI agents about the bribes, he lied, and then confessed. He also testified to having provided trucking work for the company, before the payoffs, with no expectation of money.

Why? "As a favor to the alderman," he testified.

In a surprise to court observers, the alderman was called to testify by Atty. Montgomery, not the prosecution. Acquittals in federal court are extremely rare. Once indictments are returned, the actual trial is often a foregone conclusion.

Guilty As Charged

The federal government's resources are so vast that defendants often simply plead guilty and negotiate the best deal that they can. This decision sometimes lessens the stress, but always reduces what could be astronomical legal fees, an amount of money often far beyond the reach of the ordinary citizen.

Because of the daunting odds, and the documented conviction rate in federal court, defense attorneys often urge their clients to settle, rather than go to trial.

In this case, Bolden was acquitted of extortion, convicted of filing false tax returns. He was sentenced to one year's probation, including four months house confinement.

"The government used individuals who were not very trustworthy," concluded Atty. Montgomery.

THE FULLER CASE

When the star witness in a political corruption trial is introduced with the warning, *"He is as crooked as they come,"* court observers know they are in for a bumpy ride.

Such was the prosecution's intro of longtime mole and FBI informant, **Michael Christopher**, setting the table for his testimony in the **"Operation Silver Shovel"** trial of **Thomas Fuller**, once president of the **Metropolitan Water Reclamation District**. And he was their witness.

In what some considered a surprise move, Fuller pleaded guilty to two tax charges just before jury selection in his **1998** trial. Once selected, the jury considered testimony on the remaining **ten counts** of, **extortion**, **fraud** and **racketeering**.

Asked about the guilty plea, Atty. Montgomery succinctly said, *"He pled guilty to what he was guilty of, and he pled not guilty to what he's not guilty of."*

In anticipation of the government calling Christopher to testify against his client, Atty. Montgomery characterized Christopher as a *"corrupt contractor, thief, perpetrator of multiple frauds, liar and violator of agreements he has made with the government."*

Once on the stand, Christopher testified that at least $4,000 of the $9,000 Fuller was charged with receiving from him was for assistance in getting an excavation contract from the Water Reclamation District. That contract reportedly was valued at more than $600,000.

Atty. Montgomery didn't waste time denying whether Fuller had taken money, since he was both caught on tape and later admitted his actions to FBI operatives after being confronted with the tape.

Instead, Montgomery hammered home the undeniable fact that Fuller didn't agree to and never did anything illegal in return for the money.

Ultimately, Fuller received the minimum thirty-seven month sentence and a $9,000 fine. After hiring new counsel, the conviction was confirmed on appeal.

Chapter 21

MONTGOMERY/COCHRAN FLIGHT TIME

"There wasn't a case over $10 million that we didn't fight about."

Atty. James D. Montgomery, Sr.

Atty. Johnny Cochran

By the dawn of the year **2000, Atty. James D. Montgomery, Sr.** was a success in every way one would choose to define the word.

At a time when most successful senior attorneys are counting their money and reminiscing, Atty. Montgomery was seeking new challenges.

He had excelled in every type of law that he chose to practice... **criminal defense, civil wrongful death, police shootings, municipal.**

He was a sought after legal expert in **Chicago**, and around the country. But especially in Chicago. So, when **Johnny "OJ" Cochran** looked to establish his premier brand in the *"Windy City"* that he would end up connecting with **Montgomery** was, if not inevitable, certainly understandable.

But, the merging of big money, big talent and big egos often comes with big problems.

THE BEGINNING

Big-time collaborations like this don't just happen. They occur for a reason... usually money. Atty. Montgomery explains:

> I have a friend, Bill Murphy, who lives in Baltimore, the brother of Madelyne Rabb, a colleague from the Washington administration. He called to tell me that he had talked to Johnny Cochran, who was thinking about opening an office in Chicago.

> *Bill told him, 'If you are going to Chicago, you ought to hook up with my friend Jim Montgomery.' Johnny recalled having met me at an annual meeting of the **International Academy of Trial Lawyers**.*

At some point, Cochran sends one of the firm's four partners to Chicago to negotiate an agreement with Jim Montgomery.

He recalls:

> *I had given it some thought. They were heavy on what you had to kick in to be a part of, in effect, a licensee, **The Cochran Firm**. So, I had to think seriously about it.*

> *I finally shared the idea with one of my close colleagues, **Atty. Ed Genson**, who said, 'Hell, go on and do it. He's going to generate some business.'*

> *He was absolutely right. When Johnny was alive, we attracted a lot of major cases that I would not otherwise have been able to get. Although I might have gotten some of those cases, it would have been infrequent.*

> *It all went well. Johnny was basically gallivanting all over the country, opening offices in different places. We would have annual meetings, which were feel good meetings because everything was going well.*

MONEY, MONEY, MONEY

Clashes over money are common. Often it's not much money. Here, at least to most people, the money was large. Atty. Montgomery picks up the narrative.

> *There came a time when one of the cases generated about **$14 million** gross, which meant about a **$4 million** or **$5 million** fee. Of course, Johnny then wanted to change the rules and increase his take because he went with us on the day we negotiated a settlement. The case involved a section of steel lockers at a Detroit YMCA, falling on a pre-teen boy resulting in permanent injury.*

> *Every case we had was a Cochran Firm case, except those that I had before we started. So he had every right to get about **thirty percent** of the fee. But I think he wanted **fifty percent** on this case.*

> *We almost broke up because of that situation.*

Atty. Montgomery recalls this incident as occurring very early in the relationship, probably in 2002 or 2003. Johnny Cochran passed in **2005**.

208

Permission granted by Chicago Sun-Times

His national partners encouraged him to relent a little. I was left with a very bad taste in my mouth about it.

*The **LaTanya Haggerty** case had been in my office before he showed up. I settled the case after doing two and a half years of pre-trial work. I kept it in the press every damn month so that it became a heater case and had stickup value.*

This was a controversial police shooter case, meaning there was accelerated public and media attention. City and police officials were anxious to reach a settlement, and avoid a prolonged trial and more bad publicity. Plaintiff's attorneys covet these kinds of cases because they often mean hefty fees, minus the preparation, drudgery and expense of a trial.

*I ended up settling the **Haggerty** case for $18 million, on the eve of trial. I used as a battering ram the fact that Johnny and I were going to try the case together.*

The case involved a car chase gone bad in 1999 on Chicago's South Side, resulting in the *"wrongful death"* of a young black woman, gunned down by a black female police officer, who unfortunately mistook a cell phone for a gun.

Following a thirty-one-block car chase, initiated for still undetermined reasons, Chicago police officers severely beat the male occupant/driver. However, he got off relatively easy, living to tell his story.

The passenger, LaTanya Haggerty, suffered the ultimate penalty, shot multiple times while talking on cell phone, reportedly to her mother. In a rare occurrence, the officer plus two others were later fired for their participation. A fourth officer was given a one year suspension.

LaTanya Haggerty was the youngest of three children, and the first to complete college. She was successfully working in Corporate America teaching computer skills. Her proud mother and father were not typical litigants. They demanded justice and did not define justice as mere financial compensation.

Atty. Montgomery recalls, *"When I informed them that it was customary to make a monetary demand to assess the city's inclination to settle, Mrs. Haggerty wanted no part of it. When I insisted she give me a number she said,*

209

'tell them I want $95 million.' I assured her that I would not make a demand. We decided to make no demand at all. I'm sure after the city assessed their risks following a mock trial with a jury; they were spooked by the absence of a demand."

One of the persistent criticisms lodged against the Chicago Police Department is the fact that officers rarely suffer any consequences, even in the most obvious, egregious circumstances.

Once the Haggerty family retained Atty. Montgomery, the undisputed factual circumstances of the case, resulted in settlement figures as high as $100 million being floated, even as he prepared for trial.

In **May, 2001**, once city attorneys indicated their desire to settle instead of going to trial, the family agreed to accept $18 million, payable in two equal installments.

Atty. Montgomery recalls, *"So the night before the trial date, Johnny showed up at the airport. He had a little package I had given him to read. But, I had already settled the case for $18 million before the plane landed."*

"In trying to fairly calculate his fee, I said, 'Johnny had something to do with this case. I used his good name to reel the case in.' I was thinking maybe about $200,000 for his trouble."

*"I decided to talk to **Atty. Earl Neal**, one of my close advisors. I said, 'Earl what do you think I ought to give him on this case?' After asking a few questions, he said, 'Jim, I think you ought to make it **$300,000**.' So, I made it $300,000."*

"That payment failed to satisfy Atty. Cochran. Johnny bad-mouthed me all over the firm and nationally for taking advantage of him, or some nonsense like that. He never did tell me what he wanted. But, I really didn't give a damn, because that wasn't part of our deal. The question now was do I quit, or is it worth it to stay? So, I stayed. But, it left another bad taste in my mouth."

IF IT'S NOT ONE HIGH-PROFILE CASE, IT'S ANOTHER

Recalling the last time he and Atty. Cochran worked together, Atty. Montgomery said, *"The last time we engaged together on a case, he actually came into Chicago. He sat in the office while I took depositions of **Northwestern University's** witnesses in the **Rashidi Wheeler** case. One witness was deposed by a Cochran surrogate from out of town."*

Rashidi Wheeler, an asthmatic strong safety on Northwestern's football team, collapsed and died in 2001 shortly after doing wind sprints during a voluntary preseason workout. The **NCAA** has very strict rules governing preseason voluntary practices, including the stipulations that no coaches or videotaping are allowed.

The death of Wheeler at the age of twenty-two also raised several legal issues including:

- **Should he have been participating in the drill considering his medical condition?**
- **Why was the practice taped, in violation of NCAA rules?**
- **Why was there no medical assistance available at the practice?**

Other questions, raised during pre-trial deliberations, centered on why Northwestern was never sanctioned. Some also questioned why the school never conducted an independent investigation and why **Coach Randy Walker** was never fired.

Northwestern's defense included an assertion that Wheeler had ingested prohibited performance enhancement supplements before participating in the drill. They claim that this was a contributing factor to his death.

Added to the drama was the fact that Wheeler's divorced parents initially filed petitions to be the sole representatives of their deceased son's estate. They later agreed to drop their individual efforts, however reluctantly, and work together.

Atty. Montgomery picks up the narrative:

> *Johnny had one of his associates come in, and I think he may have taken a couple of depositions. So, they did participate. Johnnie Cochran was willing to settle for $8 million, which was a number Northwestern indicated they were willing to pay.*
>
> *But, I said, 'Johnny, this is not an $8 million case. This is a stickup case. Northwestern can't afford to have this case go to trial. They can't afford to have this bad publicity.'*
>
> *So, we decided to [continue] our depositions and do our pre-trial work. By the time we finished the depositions and discovery, we ended up conferencing with a mediator. Johnny didn't participate. Once we were done with the mediator, Northwestern clearly indicated they would pay $16 million.*
>
> *Our client's mother was upset. By this time, she had fired me twice. I had returned to the case at her request. When I offered her $16 million, she fired me again. I think she had $25 million in her head. But, she really wanted justice. She didn't give a damn about the money, as much as she wanted to do something to Northwestern for killing her son. Understandably, she was a very angry lady.*

211

When she fired me the third time, I said, 'Let me tell you something. I'm not coming back. I'll just get my fee based on the value I brought to the case.'

Sure enough, she hired somebody. Later, she called me. I said, 'What's up?' She said, 'You didn't call me this time.' I said, laughing, 'Hell, it's embarrassing.'

So, the judge decided to appoint a special magistrate, a guardian ad litem, for the interests of Rashidi's brother who was a minor. This man was charged with determining whether this offer was in the best interests of this minor. He concluded that it was in his best interests.

She [the judge] was good enough to award us our contract amount. The law says that if you did the work to generate the fee, quantum meruit is the value of your services.

Even in that case, Johnny and I had a fight. There wasn't a multi-million dollar case over $10 million that we didn't fight about. So, I was a little fed up, but I was making money.

After Johnny died, realistically, I wasn't getting the volume that I was getting before. By that time we were doing pretty well. Shortly after his death in 2005 we reduced the percentage payable to The Cochran Firm to ten percent.

AND THEN?

After Cochran died, the firm was run by **Jock Smith**, an **African American attorney** from **Tuskegee, Alabama**, and two white attorneys. They made another guy, **Hezekiah Sistrunk**, from **Atlanta**, a partner.

It became clear to me that the white partners had pretty much funded the national firm at its inception, and continuing on until the dollars started rolling in. They sort of treated Jock and Sistrunk like younger brothers.

I saw that in terms of dealing with principled issues, I couldn't get any real support. So, it was a very unhappy relationship after Johnny died, and even while he was alive.

JOHNNY COCHRAN REWOUND

It's probably fair to say that before **OJ1, the double murder trial in 1994**, most people had never heard of Johnny Cochran. After the most heavily publicized trial in American judicial history, it would be hard to find anyone who didn't know him. He was forever defined by seven simple words, *"If it doesn't fit, you must acquit."*

OJ1, of course, ended with the acquittal of former football star **O.J. Simpson** in the murders of his former wife, **Nicole Brown-Simpson**, and her friend, **Ron Goldman**.

The truth is that Johnny Cochran was a highly sought-after criminal defense lawyer before **OJ1**, having defended among others, **Michael Jackson**, who had his own highly publicized legal difficulties. He got him off, as well.

Cochran helped defend Jackson against child molestation charges in another widely publicized trial that occurred just before the Simpson trial. There is some evidence that his involvement with the Jackson trial helped land him on Simpson's *"Dream Team"* of powerhouse defense attorneys.

THE MAN

As an important part of the Cochran Firm, Atty. Montgomery had the opportunity to both work with Cochran and to informally interact with him. By 2000, he was both instantly recognizable on the street, and a media celebrity.

Asked how he would describe Johnny Cochran to someone who had never met him, Atty. Montgomery said:

> *[Cochran was] one of the most amazing celebrities I had ever met. If a stranger approached him on the street, he would stop and talk with them as if they were someone that he knew. Sometimes I didn't like to go to lunch with him because it took so long to get to the restaurant.*

> *He was an amazing person in terms of not being a snob. He was someone who genuinely paid attention to people. I wish I had that skill, but I just like to get on and move on.*

"Cochran's celebrity extended beyond the streets, it also reached the courtrooms," according to Atty. Montgomery.

"When we went to the courthouse in Detroit to deal with the locker-fall-down case that we settled for $14 million…everybody – court personnel and everyone – wanted to take pictures with Johnny Cochran."

THE LAWYER

Having worked closely with Atty. Cochran over a five-year-period, Atty. Montgomery is in a unique position to speak to the characteristics that made Cochran one of the most successful attorneys of the twentieth century, along with himself.

He says:

> *He was very articulate, with a good common sense of what moves people. However, if you took Johnny Cochran and compared him with the best lawyers, using whatever criteria you want, he probably would not fully match up; but, he could probably be just as effective.*
>
> *For example, I watched the O.J. Simpson trial very carefully. I saw how he dealt with witnesses. He showed sincerity. He was a salesman. He was a guy who understood what moved people. He knew how to ingratiate himself with the jury.*

THE END

> *When Johnny was in New Orleans, on the last case (or one of the last cases he tried), he asked the jury for some ungodly sum of money $50 million. They gave him $59 million.*
>
> *So, then the jury wanted to take a picture with him. It turned out that was probably the beginning of the end, health-wise for him.*
>
> *He appeared to be limping during the trial. He went and had an evaluation. It was determined that he had an inoperable brain tumor. He actually had the tumor removed although some of the tissue remained at the margins. He ended up dying just an awful death over the period of about a year in 2005 at the age of sixty-seven.*

Currently, the Cochran firm has more than twenty offices in locations including **Detroit, Houston, Washington D.C./Baltimore, Atlanta, Birmingham, Las Vegas, Los Angeles, New York, New Orleans**, and others.

214

POSTSCRIPT

The legal game is often high stakes with liberty and/or money at risk. The big gamers often attract supporters and critics much like athletes. The question? In a big time murder trial, who would you choose between **Judge R. Eugene Pincham** and **Atty. Johnny Cochran**?

The question was posed to *Atty. Montgomery* who knew and worked with both. His answer?

"Probably Judge Pincham."

Why?

> *Gene was a skillful lawyer, both in terms of trial tactics and technique. He was a legal scholar. But, he was also a southerner who had a southern charm about himself.*
>
> *I'll never forget Gene. He'd tell some stories to the jury about how when he was a boy and his mama was 'po'. White folks go for that stuff, like a rat going for cheese.*
>
> *And, I knew more about Gene. I've tried cases with Gene. I've sat at his kitchen table and learned from Gene. So, I have a lot of admiration for his success.*
>
> *He handled cases for those who could afford to pay. And, he handled cases for those who couldn't pay. But, he worked just as hard for those who couldn't pay, as for those who could.*

215

Chapter 22
TRUSTEE MONTGOMERY

"Education is the jewel casting brilliance into the future."

Mari Evans – Poet

THE CALL

Emil Jones, Jr., an extremely savvy Democrat and influential member of Chicago's African American elite, served in the Illinois Senate from 1983 to 2009. He was the president of the Illinois Senate from 2003 to 2009.

Former Illinois Senate President Emil Jones, Jr.

The Illinois Senate has the right to approve or reject a gubernatorial appointment. So, the president of the Illinois Senate has a good deal of power. It was within the context of President Jones exercising his power that he made a call to Atty. Montgomery at the start of 2007.

He said, *"Jim, how would you like to be on the University of Illinois Board of Trustees?"* Atty. Montgomery responded *"yes"* after brief consideration.

At the time of the call, the two had been close friends for more than forty years. Their friendship started around 1966/1967 when Montgomery was a young lawyer and politician running for alderman of the 21st Ward. President Jones was an alderman's assistant.

His father, Emil Jones, Sr., a Chicago Democratic precinct captain and courtroom bailiff, had helped Atty. Montgomery navigate the courthouse as a new lawyer.

THE APPOINTMENT

At President Jones' request, Governor Rod Blagojevich appointed Atty. Montgomery, a Democrat, to the University of Illinois Board of Trustees on January 18, 2007. He filled the seat formerly held by Champaign County Republican leader, Marjorie Sodemann.

l-r: Former Illinois Governor Rod Blagojevich and Former Illinois Senate President Emil Jones, Jr.

The new trustee embraced his role. He recognized it was an opportunity to be a decision-maker at a different level.

He was uniquely positioned as someone who had been an African American student at the University of Illinois at Urbana-Champaign. He was also a graduate of the law school. He would share his experiences and perspective with the predominately white administration, which would shine a light on the huge disparities that existed on campus between white students and students of color, particularly African American students.

THE HIGHLIGHTS

Trustee Montgomery soon discovered that his time as a trustee would be anything but dull. Controversy and scandal never ceased to exist at the University of Illinois. Often resulting in irresistible media cover stories, they also served as fuel for progress.

Mandate to Retire Chief Illiniwek

Chief Illiniwek ("the Chief") was the official mascot and symbol of the University of Illinois at Urbana-Champaign. It was an important branding component to the University's intercollegiate athletic programs from 1926 to February 21, 2007.

On February 16, 2007, Lawrence Eppley, Chair of the Board of Trustees, issued a unilateral ruling retiring the Chief.

The last "official" performance, by the final Chief, Dan Maloney of Galesburg, Illinois, took place on February 21, 2007 at the last men's home basketball game of the 2006–2007 regular season against Michigan in Assembly Hall.

On March 13, 2007, the University of Illinois board of trustees voted to retire the Chief's name, image, and regalia.

President Joseph B. White supported the removal of the Chief.

Trustee Montgomery's involvement in the removal of Chief Illiniwek was an after-the-fact role because the University had been involved in that struggle before he was appointed about a month earlier.

218

Before Jim came on board as a trustee, Senate President Jones had been working to remove the Chief as the University's official mascot and symbol. He felt, as many others did, that the Chief was racist and should not represent the University of Illinois.

In his capacity as Senate president, Jones, made it known that any reappointments or new appointments were contingent on abolishing the Chief.

Dr. Frances Carroll—a senior member of the Board of Trustees at the time—was also an extremely important factor and party to the Chief's removal. Dr. Carroll joined President Jones in opposing the Chief.

As recently as 2016, University-related student organizations that are supporters of the Chief continue to have activities and annual events to encourage restoring the Chief as the University's official symbol. At the same time, there have been complaints from a professor about the inaction of the administration in enforcing the Board of Trustees' mandate that all remnants of the Chief be discontinued.

The Admissions Scandal

The University's clout/admissions scandal resulted from a series of articles in the *Chicago Tribune*, which reported that some unqualified applicants to the University of Illinois at Urbana-Champaign (UIUC) received *"special consideration"* for *acceptance* between 2005 and 2009.

The series began on May 29, 2009. As a result, a few weeks later, Illinois Governor Pat Quinn appointed an investigatory committee. The controversy led to the resignation of University President Joseph B. White, who oversaw the three campuses in the University system, as well as Chancellor Richard Herman of the Urbana-Champaign campus.

Eventually, evidence of impropriety by members of the Board of Trustees surfaced, resulting in the resignation of seven of the nine members. Trustee Larry Eppley, who served as board chairman from 2002-2008, was the first to resign. He had more admissions requests than any other member.

Trustee and Chairman of the Board Niranjan Shah was the second member to announce his resignation from the board amid allegations that he had interfered with applications and had pressured the University to hire one of his relatives. Soon after, other trustees followed. However, two trustees—Atty. Montgomery and Dr. Frances Carroll—refused to resign.

On June 10, 2009, Governor Quinn announced the appointment of a panel, led by former judge Abner Mikva, to investigate the allegations. The panel found that trustees, deans, White, and Herman all contributed to "substantial... admission-related abuses and irregularities."

219

Key elements of the panel's recommendations included:

- Calling **"on all members of the Board of Trustees to voluntarily submit their resignations and thereby permit the Governor to determine which Trustees should be reappointed."**

- Urging the Governor to **"charge the new Board with conducting a thorough and expeditious review of the University President, the UIUC Chancellor, and other University administrators, with respect to the information set forth in the Commission's Report."**

- Recommending creation of a **"firewall" that isolates school officials not involved with the admissions process.**

- Urging input on the process to elect board of trustees members from other interested parties, especially the alumni groups.

Former Illinois Governor Pat Quinn

Governor Quinn announced the following day that he would undertake the panel's recommendation and called for the resignations of all trustees.

In the wake of the admissions scandal and the panel's recommendations Trustees Montgomery and Carroll refused to resign. Trustee Montgomery explains why he refused to resign despite immense pressure to do so:

It wasn't until Quinn went to the media and called out all of us as really guilty of that process. So, I said to myself, 'If I resign, then I am admitting that I am guilty.'

Yes, I had been aware that it was going on; but I was unaware of the extent of its existence and the level at which it was organized.

Of course, I got calls like everyone else. I would call the chancellor and I would say, 'I've got a couple of very bright, young kids who I would like to see go to Illinois.' Then, he would say, 'Just have them apply, Jim.' Then, these two students just happened not to apply; so, that was on the record.

Then, there was one other instance where this guy wanted his son to go into aviation and his son's grades were not good enough to be admitted into the aviation program. So, I called the chancellor and I told him that and he said, 'Well, why don't you tell him to go to Parkland College; tell him to go there for two years; and, maybe, if he makes good grades,

220

then, maybe, he can transfer into the aviation school.' So, that's what I told the father and his son.

So, that's sort of the involvement that I had in that process. As a result, I decided not to resign and Frances Carroll also decided not to resign.

When Governor Quinn said, 'if they don't resign, then I am going to fire them.' I retained a lawyer to get prepared to sue and when the Tribune talked to me, I said, 'Not only that, if he does try to fire me I am going to file my lawsuit and fight like hell.'

Governor Quinn called Frances and me into his office with his staff. He did his best to talk us into resigning. He let us know that when his father was in the Navy, he was the captain of the ship and when things went wrong he was a part of it, stating 'and you guys were the captain of the ship.'

I said, 'Let me tell you something, this University just got a multimillion dollar grant from the government to build the most powerful computers in the world, I didn't have a damn thing to do with that and I'm not taking credit for it. By the same token, I didn't have a damn thing to do with the [admissions scandal] and I am not taking the blame; and, you went out there and bad-mouthed me, all of us.'

So, he was very disappointed and he stormed out of the room and left his staff to try to talk us out of it. Ultimately, Frances and I decided that we wouldn't resign and he didn't fire us.

It was a political decision on his part. I have a pretty good reputation in this town as does Dr. Frances Carroll. I guess he didn't want to play games. So, that was the end of that.

So, when the time came for reappointment, Quinn was still the governor. I was really enjoying being a member of the Board of Trustees and wanted to be reappointed.

I was at a meeting at Bishop Byron Brazier's church and one of the people at the meeting was University of Illinois at Chicago Chancellor Paula Allen-Meares. We were all on this committee and she said to the chairman, 'We need to do something to ensure that Mr. Montgomery gets reappointed.' So, Bishop Brazier said, 'I'll call the governor.' So, later on, Brazier called me and said, 'The governor called me back. The governor said, 'I don't see any reason why Jim should not be reappointed. He nominates Chris

[Kennedy] for chairman every year; and, I second the mo-
tion.' So, that is the way it went and Quinn reappointed me.

Now, I am the senior member of the Trustee Board because
Frances' term expired in January of 2010.

Professor Steven Salaita

In October, 2013, the University offered Steven Salaita a professorial position. However, the University withdrew the offer in 2014 after reviewing tweets of his that the University viewed as controversial.

Salaita was originally scheduled to begin in January, 2014 at the University as an associate professor with indefinite tenure as part of the American Indian Studies Program. Salaita accepted, but changed the projected start date to August 16, 2014.

On August 1, 2014, Vice President for Academic Affairs, Christophe Pierre, and Chancellor Phyllis M. Wise sent correspondence to Salaita stating that that they had chosen not to present his potential appointment to the Board of Trustees, effectively cancelling the job offer at a point after Salaita had resigned his tenured position at Virginia Tech.

Later, published e-mails between the University staff and current and former faculty, students, and community members demonstrated that the University was flooded with letters from people who objected to Salaita's controversial Twitter comments, some of which were characterized as vulgar and anti-Semitic.

Salaita asserted that the University's actions were an infringement on his academic freedom and demanded the University reinstate its job offer rather than search for a financial settlement.

Trustee Montgomery cast the only affirmative vote to reinstate Salaita's job offer. While he initially supported the withdrawal of Salaita's job offer, he believed he had been mistaken in doing so. Here, he explains why:

> *Primarily, there was an extensive legal memo written by*
> *a University of Illinois law professor. That memo sold me.*
> *What it said was that at the University, state law requires*
> *the board of trustees to approve any hiring. It is the law*
> *and it has to be that way.*

> *However, our process was such that we vet our professor*
> *hires through our deans and departments. Then, it goes*
> *to the provost. After the provost, it goes to the chancellor;*
> *and, in Salaita's case, that process actually occurred.*

Salaita was approved all the way up the line. He was told that he was approved and that he could postpone until August, 2014. So, he has every reason to believe that he has a job. So, he quits his tenured position, coming to another tenured position.

Then, the board meets after the news comes out about his tweets and we fire him; we don't hire him.

Ultimately, the judge's decision to rule in favor of Salaita rested on the University's recognized past practice of serving as a rubber stamp for the administration. The University's decision to revoke Salaita's job offer cost Illinois taxpayers more than $2 million, including an $875,000 settlement that trustees approved in November, 2015.

Professor James William Kilgore

During the 1960s, while a student at the University of California, Santa Barbara, James William Kilgore became involved with the Symbionese Liberation Army (SLA). The main SLA members were arrested in 1975. After that, Kilgore fled America for twenty-seven years. He spent most of that time in Africa. While living as a fugitive, Kilgore rejected the politics of violence. Ultimately, he established a career as an educator, researcher, and activist in Zimbabwe and South Africa. During that time, he also authored books and academic articles under the pseudonym John Pape.

In 2002, he was arrested in Cape Town, South Africa and extradited to the United States. Consequently, he served six and a half years in prison in California. During his incarceration he wrote several novels, including *We Are All Zimbabweans Now*, which was published a month after his release in 2009 by Umuzi Publishers of Cape Town.

In 2009, Kilgore began teaching at the University of Illinois at Urbana-Champaign. However, in 2014, Kilgore's employment at the University came under threat when an architect, planning the new local jail, started a campaign to pressure the University of Illinois to refuse to renew Kilgore's contract as a lecturer and academic hourly employee, primarily because of his criminal background, of which the University was aware when they initially hired him.

The withdrawal of Kilgore's employment offer prompted protests as well as the signing of a petition from faculty members and others to have his employment restored.

In November, 2014, the University of Illinois' Board of Trustees voted not to ban Kilgore from further employment, thus opening the door for him to be re-hired. As a result, he began working again in January, 2015 as a research scholar at the University of Illinois at Urbana-Champaign Center for African Studies.

The path to voting not to ban Kilgore from further employment was difficult. The end result was the product of an extremely difficult discussion amongst the Board of Trustees about redemption and diversity. Atty. Montgomery explains:

> *One of the most important discussions the trustees have had was about a man who was a criminal. He had been with the Symbionese Liberation Army. Nevertheless, he had been on the faculty for four years and was doing very well. He had a terrible background. He had done bad things. A policeman was killed as a result of a robbery he participated in when he was a member of that group. He had escaped to Africa where he earned a Ph.D., etc.*
>
> *So, that was a real, real tough, honest, and straight-up discussion. I won that argument. I told the other trustees that as a black man—and most of the people in prison are black—I was not prepared to say that someone couldn't be redeemed. That was one of my finest hours.*

THE IMPACT

Trustee Montgomery is a fierce and vocal opponent of myriad forms of racism that exist at the University. As a statesman, he brandishes diplomacy and respectability to engage an administration that—for the most part—does not take into consideration how its decisions and policies impact African American people.

Former Trustee, Dr. Frances Carroll states:

> *Certainly his presence on the board has brought about an awareness that African American students who go to the University of Illinois need support and that the rules and regulations of the University must clearly state that they include all students; and that any form of racism or prejudice is unacceptable to not only African American students, but all students of color.*
>
> *So, his knowledge of the law was so helpful. He stated the causes and the problems in a way that everyone could accept it. He was not confrontational. He would just explain the reasons why all students should have the same opportunities, and not just students, but also current and prospective personnel.*

224

Whenever they were going to recruit coaches for the basket-ball team or the football team and even for the top administra-tive positions, he and I would always recommend an African American. This helped to keep the issue of a lack of African American staff at the University within the board's sight.

Former Trustee and Board Chair, Niranjan Shah expounds:

As First Chair of the Buildings and Grounds (Facilities) Committee, and later as Board Chair, I often referred to Jim's advisement on the Board. Jim was always calm, thoughtful, and poised. And, any time he reacted, his words were full of wisdom. He cared greatly about diversity in terms of contracts, recruit-ment and admissions, and he advocated for fairness. Jim emphasized the idea that we, as a public university, especially a land grant university that is to some extent supported by public funds, had to maintain the highest standards but also be inclusive.

I knew Jim during the Harold Washington administration, when he was corporation counsel for the City of Chicago. He was part of a big change happening in the City in the early 1980s. While he is not small in stature, he has a big personali-ty that far exceeds that. I was honored when he was appointed to the Board. It was easier for me to communicate with him. When I became Board Chair, he always supported new ideas. When we all went through the turmoil in 2009, he was as steady as a rock.

Jim had tremendous impact because of his advocacy to increase diversity not only with the students and faculty, but also with contract support. For example, prior to 2002, fifty percent of the contract value for goods and services went to ten percent of the firms qualified to do the work. With Jim's support, in 2009 that percentage increased to seventy percent of contracts going to the top thirty to thirty-five percent of firms, with significant awards going to small and minori-ty-owned businesses. With his strong legal background, Jim was not afraid to try new things and advocated for how to do things differently to open the doors to people who had been shut out of the system for a long time. With his advice and counsel, it was safe to do so.

In 2009, the Chicago Tribune began talking about the admissions emails and the indictment of Governor Blagojevich. The State of Illinois was going through tremendous challenges. I desired to protect the University as Board Chair. Governor Quinn asked other trustees to step down. Everyone did except Jim Montgomery and Dr. Frances Carroll, who stood firm like a rock. They didn't step down despite the storm. They showed tremendous courage through the thunderstorms and lightning. I greatly admired their courage, and wished I had courage like that.

Trustee Jill B. Smart elaborates:

I am a big fan of Atty. Montgomery and, as I have gotten to know him, I have become a bigger and bigger fan.

He fulfills a very unique role on the board. He contributes a great deal. He doesn't necessarily speak a lot; but when he says something, you really listen because he's very insightful in the way he articulates his points of view. He has this way of drawing you in so you really want to listen. He doesn't repeat himself, which I love.

He is open to someone with whom he doesn't agree. If he does not agree with someone's point of view, he can articulate why not in a very diplomatic and respectful way.

Despite racism's persistent indignation toward the relentless advocacy and work of people like Trustee Montgomery, African Americans continue to break barriers and gain ground.

In the spring of 2016, the University hired former Chicago Bears head coach, Lovie Smith, as its first African American head Illini football coach.

Trustee Patricia Brown Holmes provides perspective regarding Atty. Montgomery's impact on the University's hiring of Lovie Smith:

Jim Montgomery comes from a background where he experienced discrimination while at the University of Illinois, as have I. We have very similar experiences, but they are decades apart, which is a shame. So, the two of us, along with others, have been advocates for diversity within the University

specifically with the coaching staff, faculty, as well as the ranks at the University of Illinois at all levels.

It makes it easy when you have an ally who has Atty. Montgomery's stature to make your point. I think that having the right viewpoints and the right tone at the top has been important. It started with Chris Kennedy, who was chair of the Board of Trustees when I came onto the Board.

Chris Kennedy always made diversity a part of the agenda. He wanted to know that every department that gave a report had considered diversity in whatever it was that they were reporting. And, so, that continued and began to permeate the Board.

As a result, it then became easier when President Killeen arrived. The Board had a viewpoint and a tone. The tone was all about diversity and President Timothy Killeen was mostly selected based on his tone about diversity. So, from the beginning, he understood that diversity was important to the Board. I think that then helped down the line.

Jim Montgomery was extremely vocal about the need to have African Americans at all levels. Particularly when it came to our coaching staff. We were one of the only universities in the Big Ten never to have had an African American head football coach or an African American head basketball coach. So, that became a focal point.

I think that is one of the reasons that Lovie Smith was eventually chosen. We got the right people in place who understood the mission. A lot of that was because Jim Montgomery was very vocal about it.

Atty. Montgomery's term as a member of the University of Illinois Board of Trustees is set to expire in 2019.

INTERVIEW WITH CHRISTOPHER G. KENNEDY

Christopher G. Kennedy served as chairman of the Board of Trustees at the University of Illinois from 2009 to 2015.

In the following interview, Mr. Kennedy provides insight into his personal and professional relationship with Atty. Montgomery. He also discusses periods that were important to him and the other trustees involved.

227

Duties of a Trustee

Jim was one of two trustees not removed by Governor Quinn after the Category I admissions scandal. Jim had been part of the Board, but had refused to step down, making it clear that he had done nothing wrong. This forced me to confront, in a deeper way, the duties of a trustee. I thought about it, I wrote about it, and I ultimately spoke about it, and those thoughts were inspired by Jim.

The fundamental question, I believe, was this—are the trustees on the Board to serve the best interests of the University, the best interests of the Governor who appointed them, the best interests of themselves, or the best interests of the people of the state? Through Jim's example, I recognized that there can only be one answer to this question—we must each serve as a fiduciary there to represent the owners, which are the people of Illinois. Jim had done this when he stood up to Governor Quinn, and he continued to do it time and again as we served together.

My First Meeting

Our first meeting together was held in Urbana-Champaign. Jim welcomed me to the dinner. The dinner itself could have been an awkward affair, but his graciousness and charm showed through, and he made me feel welcome. Late that night, we spoke, and he offered to put my name in nomination for the chairmanship the next day. Many of the mechanics of the meeting I thought had been worked out by the Governor's office, but that was not true. Jim and I then scrambled to put together a slate of officers and committee assignments. We could easily have isolated the minority Republicans on the Board, but Jim was thoughtful about trying to use each person's unique assets and background in service to the University.

Leadership Resignations

We faced a series of resignations, including those from the President of the University at the time, Joe White, and the Chancellor of the Urbana campus, Richard Herman. Their culpability in the admissions scandal was difficult to gauge, given the enormous pressure they were subject to from Governor Blagojevich's office and through Governor Blagojevich's intermediaries.

I spoke often with Jim during this time to sort through opposing viewpoints and to confirm the sequence of various events. I never felt the need to review prior board minutes from the Executive Sessions because I always had great faith in Jim's recollections and honest judgement about all of these things.

Bill Ayers

We faced a crisis in our efforts to restore a working relationship with the Board of Trustees and the faculty leadership when Bill Ayers' name was put in nomination for emeritus status.

I discovered this proposal very deep in the back of hundreds of pages of board material. Jim was one of the first people I spoke with to try and sort out the obligations of the trustees. He helped me sort through what was properly personal and, therefore, had no place in decision-making at a board level and what part of our existence as people of our time should rightly inform our decisions.

I assume, but have no proof, that many other board members sought Jim's guidance and advice, and we came together with a unanimous vote. The faculty was understanding and often supportive, and the relationship with alumni and other supporters was greatly enhanced.

Authors' Note: Bill Ayers is a retired professor in the College of Education at the University of Illinois at Chicago and former leader in the counterculture movement that opposed the United States' participation in the Vietnam War. The Board of Trustees voted unanimously to deny Bill Ayers emeritus status.

Stan Ikenberry

Joe White suggested we bring Stan Ikenberry in as an interim president while we conducted a search. I had not known Stan, and I was concerned about the notion that we might be perpetuating tarnished leadership. I spoke with Jim, and he assured me that we would be lucky to have Stan Ikenberry and that Stan's presence as an interim president would instantly provide credibility to the Board and to the University. Jim was right, and the decision to bring Ikenberry back was one of the best decisions the Board made.

Authors' Note: Stanley O. Ikenberry served as the fourteenth president of the University of Illinois. He retired from the University presidency in 1995, but returned in 2010 to serve as interim president.

Reforms

We quickly adopted a series of reforms, which Jim was helpful in conceiving. There were so few of us who had a deeper understanding of the operations of the University that we had to rely on him. We reduced the number of committees, we increased the president's authority, and we changed the title to add Chief Executive to clearly signify our respect for the position. We clarified reporting relationships, where the President reports to the Board but everyone else reports to the President. We also shared our dedication to this mission with the important constituents, including the Foundation and the Alumni Association, in public and open settings.

Mike Hogan

In the final throes of the Board's deliberations regarding Mike Hogan, [former chancellor of the University of Iowa and the president who immediately preceded the current president], I summed up a position I thought informed a majority of the Board, which was that, at that time, Mike Hogan was the risk-free choice, given the more junior and untested candidates who were part of the final pool. There was, perhaps, no sentence I could have uttered which would have been more damaging to Jim's opinion of a candidate. He offered a vigorous rebuttal, not of Mike Hogan so much but instead of the notion that we should be guided by making "risk-free choices." It was a great lesson to me at that meeting, and it continued to reverberate throughout my thinking for the remainder of my term on the Board. Jim made it clear that we were put on this earth for something greater than avoiding risks.

Authors' Note: Michael Hogan, former president of the University of Connecticut, was selected in the spring of 2010—after the Clout Scandal ended Joe White's presidency—to serve as the University of Illinois' president. From the start of his presidency, Hogan had an extremely contentious relationship with the University of Illinois faculty. Ultimately, he resigned his position as the University of Illinois' president in the summer of 2012.

Dismissal of Tenured Professor Lou Wozniak

The trustees had no record of any prior experience at the University of Illinois related to removing tenure from a sitting faculty member. This had the potential to be damaging to the University and to the Board's relationship with the faculty. Jim's efforts to ensure that the Board was fully informed of the events that led to the matter coming before us was instrumental in helping us find a path forward.

230

Jim's own experience in court and his unwavering sense of justice helped shape a process that we felt did the most to protect the property right to tenure that has been enshrined in individual faculty members. No one was happy or proud of the outcome, but we were confident that we had developed a process which ultimately protected our students as well as individual faculty members.

Authors' Note: In the fall of 2013, board members voted unanimously to fire hugely popular, tenured engineering professor, Lou Wazniak. They made their decision after an administration report demonstrated that Wozniak's misconduct "badly damaged the university's paramount mission of trust and support for its students."

Labor

The University is a signatory to its scores of labor agreements. Jim was often asked to lead the Board's efforts in sorting through some of the unfamiliar language and arcane concepts, which govern our relationships with the team at the University of Illinois, and, more importantly, they determine the quality of life for thousands of employees. Jim's expertise in this area was well-known, and he was asked to take on leadership roles representing the University and other institutions on state boards that determined the fate of the lives of hundreds of thousands of people.

Diversity

Jim helped focus the Board on the University's efforts around diversity. At each of the six regularly scheduled board meetings, the subject of diversity in some aspect of the University was added to the agenda for highlight and discussion. Jim organized a retreat for the Board around the notion of diversity. It was, for the participants, one of the most challenging meetings any of us had participated in. Each and every one of us who was lucky enough to be there came away from the meetings thinking it was one of the most transformational events in our life.

Chapter 23

JUDGES, LAWYERS, AND COLLEAGUES SHARE THEIR REFLECTIONS

"The guy who takes a chance,
who is unafraid of failure, will succeed."

Gordon Parks – Photographer – Author – Film Director

WALTER JONES, JR., ESQ.

How did you meet?

 *I met Jim at the end of 1969 and the beginning of 1970. I was working on a senior trial project while in law school. The instructor, who later became a federal judge, decided that my trial partner—who was also African American—and I ought to have access to the few black lawyers in Chicago. So, he assigned Jim to assist us with our trial project.*

I thought it was the experience of a lifetime because if you go back to the stats, even in 1972, there were only 4,000 African American lawyers in the United States. I was getting an opportunity to meet someone who was at the top end of his profession and I was awed by the experience.

What did you glean from the experience that was useful in your career?

I later became and have been a significant trial lawyer in this town. Jim's tutoring at the time was on how best to give opening statements and cross-examine witnesses. These are the qualities that have always made Jim better than anybody else. So, I think I came away with a positive experience.

How would you describe Montgomery in a few words?

Dynamic, energetic...this is very easy for me because the moment Jim enters a courtroom or anything that he is either in charge of or has anything significant to do with, the moment he opens his mouth, everyone knows that he is someone special. He is a dynamic presence who makes people stand up and take notice.

Have you ever witnessed him in a trial?

Yes, both with and against him.

When Jim was one of the directors of Highland Bank, I was brought in to assist in the big fight with a very powerful group that wanted to take over the bank. There was a significant dispute and we were in trial and I had to work with Jim. Of course, Jim was the overseer. I mean he did everything you would expect a great lawyer to do. His everyday advice, his counsel, his grasp of the law are things that he has garnered over all the years he has been practicing law. Yes, we won! We beat them up so badly that the case had gone on for several years and when we finished with them, after several days of trial, they decided that it was in their best interest to settle.

How was it going up against him?

Well, this is one that Jim would always like to forget. The reason that there is no death penalty in Illinois is because there was a case where there had been an individual, Anthony Porter, who had been incarcerated for sixteen years on death row. After Mr. Porter had been on death row for sixteen years, he got a pardon of innocence by Governor George Ryan. Governor Ryan would go on to suspend all death penalty cases in Illinois. Well, the moment that Anthony Porter got out of jail, he hired Jim Montgomery and they sued the City of Chicago for twenty-four million dollars. We went to trial on that case and I am happy to say that the jury came back with zero.

On Jim's fiftieth anniversary in the law practice, I was one of the speakers. So, I got up...you know Jim is one who has won millions of dollars in verdicts. So, I had fun. So, I said, "Jim glad to see that, but what about Porter?"

Do you currently have a professional relationship with Montgomery?

I would say that [my firm] has represented Jim and his firm on several matters. So, I would still say yes.

Also, Jim is still sort of my boss because in this huge University of Illinois coaching controversy, my firm was fortunate enough to represent the University of Illinois in this situation. Of course, Jim is a trustee at the University of Illinois.

What is your overall reflection on his career?

It seems to me that not only did Jim bring the best talent to the ball game, but he also brought the best work ethic to the ball game. When you have those two elements and you have not lost your ability—even with age—to convey both of those, then you are still going to whip most of the people in the game.

I have seen him for over forty some years now. He and a guy named R. Eugene Pincham, when I used to be chief of the criminal division for the federal prosecutor's office here in this town. Those two guys were our nemeses. The moment when I saw Jim and Eugene's names on the pleading, I would just look up and tell everybody, "Okay, you got to rise to a different level because this is an entirely new ball game.

234

LEWIS MYERS, JR. ESQ.

How did you meet Atty. Montgomery?

I have known of Jim Montgomery since the early 1970s. I worked with Professor Herbert Reid who was a former dean of Howard Law School and who taught me at Rutgers Law School.

I worked on a project involving the investigation between law enforcement and the Black Panther Party. One of the things we worked on was the Fred Hampton shooting. Professor Reid was the head of the project and I was one of his student assistants.

I had come to Chicago and we were investigating the Panthers shoot down and that was when I first learned of Jim Montgomery. His name came to my attention while working with that project. With a lot of people who worked in Chicago who were doing similar human rights work, the name Montgomery came up over and over again.

So, when I moved to Chicago in 1980, I came here to represent Larry Hoover, who was indicted and charged with capital murder for allegedly killing three white prison guards at Pontiac Prison. That was my first real opportunity to meet Jim.

Jim knew of me because I was a civil rights lawyer down in Mississippi. I had tried a lot of cases all over the country.

I remember when I first came to Chicago, Jim had a speaking engagement because his son and his daughter were going to the University of Illinois' Law School in Champaign. He gave me the compliment of asking me to go down and speak to the black law students down in Champaign, the University of Illinois Law School, because he could not make it.

We have had a great, great relationship over the years. I know his family. I have worked with him now for a number of years.

What word or phrase best describes him?

Jim is an excellent trial lawyer. I think that any lawyer who stands in the courtroom in the presence of Jim Montgomery cannot help but learn. He has achieved excellence in the field of trial litigation. The other word is respect. He is a person of respect and integrity. I admire his level of integrity and respect. The way he treats other human beings. And, most importantly, he has a sincere dedication to fighting for the rights of African Americans across this country.

What experience do you have working with him?

I worked with Jim on cases over the years. Some of them have been quite public cases. He and I worked on cases involving Minister Farrakhan and the Nation of Islam. And, most recently, a case involving a politician here in Chicago.

I have had an opportunity to work with him on cases over the last twenty-five or thirty years and I have always been in a learning mode. To work with Jim Montgomery is really a part of a process of learning and growing in excellence and achievement.

One of the most important things that I have experienced in working with him is that he has a vast wealth of knowledge. He also has tremendous commitment to causes he believes. And, most importantly, as an attorney, he has an excellent command of facts and circumstances compared to other people.

The only other person I have encountered in my career whom I grew to love and admire with such a command of people and experiences and passion was R. Eugene Pincham. Nevertheless, Jim Montgomery is truly a person who has the compassion and love for what he does, love for his community, and love of the work he has been involved with over the years. For that, he is a model person.

Are there any case(s) that stand out as remarkable?

Some of them are still ongoing.

Let me just put it this way… for fourteen years, I was the National General Counsel for the Nation of Islam. I have been a private lawyer for Louis Farrakhan now for forty-two years. I have traveled all over the world on behalf of the Nation and representing Minister Farrakhan. A lot of what I have done and a lot of the cases that I have been involved with, absolutely Jim Montgomery has also been involved with.

I can give you one case back some years ago. The Nation of Islam had received a grand jury subpoena about a murder down in Houston, Texas. Jim and I traveled to Houston together. We had clients and members of the Nation of Islam who were targets of investigation involving the Houston murder trial. He and I worked extensively on that case, including preparing a couple of Nation of Islam members to appear before the grand jury. That was in early 1982.

That just shows you how far we go back. That was a major case because the implication was that somehow the Nation of Islam in Chicago had been involved in the murder of one of their followers down in Houston.

236

What accounts for his longevity in the practice?

Jim's integrity and commitment account for his longevity in the practice. He is a very practical, very real person.

He has a keen sense of consciousness about who he is as an African American. He has a keen sense of consciousness about the plight and struggle of African American lawyers in America over the years. And, he brings that dynamic to his relationships with people.

I was just terribly impressed with him. As a young lawyer, I was looking for a role model and Jim Montgomery was an excellent role model. I am proud to say that in trying cases over the years, much of what I learned and a lot of the achievements I have accomplished, have been because I had a role model like Jim Montgomery to follow. I think that is very important.

Will you share your involvement with the National Conference of Black Lawyers Fred Hampton School of Law and International Diplomacy?

Jim Montgomery also taught at the school and we interacted in that. I worked with the Fred Hampton School of Law because I used to work for the National Conference of Black Lawyers out of New York City.

At one point, I was the general counsel for the National Conference of Black Lawyers. Our office was up in Harlem and I worked all over the country. So, when I decided to move to Chicago in 1980 to represent Larry Hoover, I was already a friend with an individual by the name of Charles Knox.

Charles Knox was a former Black Panther Party member who had graduated from DePaul University's Law School. He then decided in 1975 to found a black law school, here in Chicago at 4545 S. Drexel. I maintained contact with Charles Knox. He and I worked on a number of projects with the National Conference of Black Lawyers out of New York.

When I came to Chicago, Charles Knox extended me the invitation to teach and work at the law school, while I was here representing Larry Hoover. I accepted and taught classes at the school.

Jim Montgomery was also a professor at the law school. Over a period of years, I think the law school did make an impact. It was a center of education and learning. And it was a center for education and learning that was key toward developing revolutionary and progressive black lawyers.

At the time, we realized that there was a need and a void in America when it came to black lawyers involving themselves in controversial and political cases. We did not have a lot of black lawyers who were at the forefront that the public knew about.

We wanted to train young, African American lawyers to be dedicated to the service of their communities and to give back to what our people had given to them. Out of that came the National Conference of Black Lawyers Fred Hampton School of Law and International Diplomacy.

Charles Knox had known Fred Hampton and had worked with Fred Hampton. Charles Knox, the founder, along with David Hammond, were co- founders of the law school. The law school was very important. It existed for a number of years and made tremendous contributions to Chicago's African American community. It certainly was influential for the people who graduated from that law school, some of whom went on to practice law.

I taught there in 1980 when I got to Chicago. As soon as I came to town, I started working with the law school. Prior to that, I had an association with the law school before I even moved here because I knew about it, and I was supportive of what they were doing. But my first time in Chicago was 1980.

THOMAS MARSZEWSKI, ESQ.

When did you first meet Atty. Montgomery?

I first met Jim in August of 1991. I was looking for a law clerk position. Jim had listed a job posting in the Chicago Kent's Legal Directory, which was where law students went to look for job listings.

Jim was actually in the office that day and sort of convinced me that he was retired, because it was August and he likes to go on his boat in August.

We immediately hit it off because despite a lot of differences—with me being Polish and Jim being African American—we had one thing in common; we were both sons of butchers. We have a similar sense of humor and a good work ethic. We come from modest backgrounds.

Then, he did a kind of FDR, Franklin Delano Roosevelt, on me. FDR was famous for giving several different people—without them knowing—the same assignment to see what people would come back with. Jim did that to a couple of students and me. I think he must have liked my answer to the question even though he did not like the answer. It was against the client he was representing, but at least it was the correct answer.

How would you describe him?

Jim is always, in terms of preparing legal cases, very thoughtful, very thorough, and very well prepared, and always seems to have fun with it.

238

I don't know if that makes sense; but a lot of lawyers just do it for work, but he actually doesn't do it just for work. It is sort of also his hobby. He just loves it and he really finds the challenges as the best part of it.

What area(s) of the law did you practice while at Montgomery's firm?

When I first started with him, for the first few years, we were the corporation counsel for the City of Harvey and Jim also did a number of criminal cases. I was his trial co-counsel on four cases and three of them were in federal court.

So, yeah, before we met Johnny Cochran, we were doing mostly civil defense and criminal. We also started to do some personal injury on a fairly limited basis, about three or four years before we partnered with Johnny Cochran.

What was it like to work with Atty. Montgomery?

Once Jim knew a case was going to trial, he was a fierce competitor. He was very well prepared. He expected me to be well prepared. He was a great taskmaster. But also, once you were in trial with him, you learned so much about how to approach things that it really made you learn quite a bit.

Jim is terrific in both direct examinations and cross-examinations, but I think he is probably one of the most fun people to watch in trial on a cross-examination because he knows what the answer is going to be before the witness does. He is not going to ask a question that he does not know the answer to on cross-examination, for the most part. There will be some exceptions to that and you just roll with it.

Jim is really one of the very few people in Chicago who can mesmerize a jury, not only in examinations, but also particularly in closing arguments, which he always loved to give and loved to prepare for.

It amazed me how time after time he could get so energized and worked up and nervous and competent at the same time, because I think he cared so much about doing well for the clients. It really wasn't about him; it was about the clients. I think that's what sets him apart from a lot of people is how much he really cares.

Now, there are a lot of amazingly talented lawyers in our town. But I think he brings a theatrical quality to the courtroom that is rare. He can send chills down your spine at the appropriate times, depending on the type of case it is.

We don't—as lawyers—always have the luxury of having the greatest cases in the world. So, not all cases are the same. In some cases you are going to do better than in others. It is not because of the lawyer; but sometime it is because of the facts. He was always very fond of saying, 'If you have great facts, then go with them and do the best you can. If you don't, then you just have to continue to work at being your best and the best lawyer you can be.' If someone says, as a lawyer, that they have won all of their cases, that means they have not tried many. Mr. Montgomery is someone who has not shied away from extremely difficult cases.

Criminal defense cases, in particular, are very difficult to win, especially at the federal level, because they have all of these tape recordings and all of this evidence at their disposal.

But, I can say that one of the cases that we had fond memories of working together on was John Bolden, a City of Chicago water commissioner. We tried the case in September of 1997 and we won the case on the theory of entrapment.

John Bolden was a water commissioner, but really not a politician. He got involved in the case because the senior African American dean of the City Council introduced him to this government mole. So, we based our defense on the Theory of Entrapment. The judge allowed us to have the instruction and we won.

What sets Atty. Montgomery apart from other lawyers?

What makes Jim special are the talents that God gave him in terms of his outlook on life and what he has been through; his humility and competence. His voice. He has a great baritone voice. He has a great sense of humor, but also a great amount of deference to the court. He is a well-respected statesman. He really presents himself professionally and has earned the respect of his peers.

To me, he is almost larger than life as a mentor. I think a lot of people will say that he was a mentor, but for me, he really was. I don't like practicing law as much as I did with him. Every day was fun.

ELVIN E. CHARITY, ESQ.

When did you initially meet Atty. Montgomery?

I first met Jim in 1985 when he was the corporation counsel for the City of Chicago under Mayor Harold Washington and I had accepted a position as chief assistant corporation counsel, heading up the real estate division of the city law department.

I had been offered the job by one of Jim's deputies, Wayne Robinson. When I accepted the position I met with Jim who took me in to meet with Harold Washington, which in and of itself was an experience.

I had never met Mayor Harold Washington. So, it was really an awesome experience, getting a chance to meet both Jim, whom I had heard a lot about, and the Mayor, whom I had obviously heard a lot about. So, that was my introduction to Jim and, obviously, I was impressed with both of them for their intellect and, really, their sense of toughness. That was the pervasive thing about Jim as I got to know him.

Then, I started working for Jim. Obviously, that was an interesting experience for me. I came out of private practice and had never really worked in government before. I was with a big law firm. During that time it was very difficult because that was when they had the twenty–nine to twenty-one majority lined up against the Mayor. So, everything we did was under very strict scrutiny. We had to be very careful and diligent about everything that we did.

Two anecdotal things about Jim. I had just started at the Law Department and I remember getting called into Jim's office. There were a group of us called in to brief him on something. I cannot even remember what it was. I was still somewhat intimidated by the whole government experience.

Jim had a big conference room table in his office. He would sit at the head of the table and the rest of us would sit around the table. Jim had these eyeglasses. They were reading glasses and they would kind of sit low on his nose. He would peer over the top rim of the glasses at you. Sometimes he would look down and either take notes or read something.

So, we were there to brief him on something or a series of things. All I remember—and again, I had been there all of maybe a month—is that one of the lawyers started going off on a tangent, starting to talk about some nonsense. It was clear that this lawyer was not prepared for what Jim wanted him to present. So, after the guy finished, Jim looked down over those glasses at him and said, 'You don't know what the fuck you're talking about.'

Jim will deny this, even today, but it is indelibly imprinted in my mind because I had only been there for like a month. So, what it taught me was that you do not go into a meeting with this man unprepared. So, from that day on, if I had a meeting with Jim Montgomery, I went into the meeting making sure that I was overly prepared. So, that is kind of my experience with Jim.

Something else about Jim. I remember being privy to conversations that he would have with Alderman Ed Burke, who was one of the leaders of the 29-21 that were against Harold Washington. Jim would be on the phone with Burke—who was chairman of the Finance Committee—and, then, in the middle of the conversation, Jim would launch into a tirade with Ed Burke and they would go back and forth.

Years later after Jim left the law department, one of the people who called him and was really sorry to see him go was Ed Burke. I think that even though they were on opposite sides of the political spectrum, Ed Burke respected Jim for his intellect and his toughness. Those are the two things that kind of characterize Jim in my mind.

I can tell another story about Jim. I grew up in the big firm practice. That's how I started, at a big firm; and, then I spent some time in government, then I went back to the big firm. And, then, I ultimately went out on my own. I now have a small, five-lawyer law firm. I remember when I first started I was negotiating on a line of credit. Working with some people, I put together a business plan. I went to a couple of banks and I wound up getting a line of credit to help me until I could start generating positive cash flow. Then, I got a small term loan to help me buy some equipment.

I remember how key this line of credit was because when I first started I had no cash. I had to generate cash flow over time by getting some business and doing some work and then over time, ultimately, billing and getting paid.

So, I remember walking through one of the tunnels in the city that connected various buildings in the city. I went to get my shoes shined. When I walked over to the shoeshine place, Jim was sitting in the chair. So, I sat up next to Jim and I said, 'I don't know how I would have managed starting my practice had I not had this line of credit.' And, Jim looked at me and said, 'You know Elvin, I never really had a line of credit because I have always had to come out of pocket.'

I was stunned because here is a guy who is one of the most prominent attorneys in the city. He's been in business, at that time, for well over twenty years and he had never had a line of credit. And here I am, just starting and I was able to get a line of credit.

It made me realize how difficult it was when guys like Jim came out of law school. They did not have the opportunities, like I had, to go to work for the big downtown firm, because that was not available to them at that time.

So, they had to go out there on their own, on their own dime, with no support to start something and build something. That again, was a telling thing to me to come out and be so successful; but to have to start totally on your own. That's not just Jim, that's a lot of the guys who were his contemporaries. They had to do it on their own dime.

Working with Jim and having a chance to just talk to him about stuff was educational. It really made me appreciate the foundation that they laid for the rest of us. I was very blessed to have mentors such as Jim and Earl Neal.

JUDGE DANIEL LOCALLO

When did you meet James Montgomery?

I first met Jim when I was a prosecutor in the State's Attorney's Office. So, it would have been around the beginning of 1980s. I was in the Cook County's Prosecutor's Office. Jim was doing defense.

How would you describe him?

I would say very thorough, well prepared. He has a very unique voice. If he calls you, it is almost as if God is talking. He is very meticulous. He enunciates his words. He is very clear. He really has a good presence. He fights hard for his clients. He is very hard working, diligent, knows his cases, the strengths and weaknesses.

Jim is [a] well-respected person. He is a man of high integrity. He is very professional in his dealings with attorneys and judges. He is hard working and also creative.

I will give you an example. I presided over a case where Jim was representing three individuals who were suing the City of Chicago and some police officers for malicious prosecution. The individuals were originally convicted of murder and eventually an individual came forward and told the FBI that others were responsible for the murder. The State's Attorney's Office dropped the charges against the three who were already in prison, convicted of murder. As a result of them being released, Jim represented them in their suit against the police and the City of Chicago. Jim actually had a replica of the jail cell created for the purposes of the jury trial. I thought that was quite creative.

It was creative and impactful. Jim actually won a nice verdict of $6.75 Million.

Jim is an outstanding attorney and he is really a person who is a good example of what attorneys are to be. Passionate in their representation of their client and at the same time, flexible with the ability to deal with their opponents. Also, the ability to deal with judges.

In the criminal case that I had, Jim was defending an individual who was involved in the shooting of Wayne Messmer (guy who sings the National Anthem). Messmer had been shot in the throat. It was an attempted robbery and Jim was representing, not the shooter, but an individual who was part of the plan to rob Messmer. Wayne Messmer was probably one of the best witnesses I have ever seen in court.

The defense was identification and every time Jim would ask him a question about the height, the weight, the lighting, etc., Wayne Messmer who was pret-

ty well prepped would answer, 'I will never forget the face of the man who shot me.' Then, Jim, at some point, said 'I bet you'd answer that way to any question I ask you.' In this case, the jury found his client guilty. But it was not due to a lack of Jim's ability or lack of diligence in representing his client. The facts, in that case, happened to favor the prosecution. Jim, as far as I am concerned, is one of the better attorneys in our system.

GINO L. DIVITO, ESQ.

When did you meet James Montgomery?

I met Jim during the 1960s and through the 1970s when I was an assistant state's attorney, a prosecutor, and, he was primarily involved with criminal defense work.

How would you describe him?

"Perfect Gentleman" is the best phrase. He was always proper, civil, friendly, outgoing and, obviously, very competent.

Have you ever worked with or against him on a case?

My most recent involvement with Jim was in our joint support for Justice Bertina Lampkin for the position of appellate court justice. Justice Lampkin is on the Illinois Appellate Court as an appointee and must run in order to retain that position and Jim and I are co-chairs of her effort to prevail in that election. So, I have dealt with Jim in that connection; and, also most recently I have acted as an expert witness in a case brought by Jim's firm against the City of Chicago, its police officers. At one time I was deposed by Jim Montgomery, Jr., his son. I need to say that I was very impressed with his son. He truly is a wonderful reflection of his father; again, a very gentlemanly and competent lawyer.

JUDGE WALTER WILLIAMS, RETIRED

How long have you known Atty. Montgomery, Sr.?

We have known each other for over forty years. I initially met Jim at either a meeting of the Cook County Bar Association or at 26th and California, which is the Criminal Courts Building. At that time, Jim was an established criminal defense attorney.

I was a young lawyer at that time, practicing criminal defense.

Did you have a role in the Cook County Bar Association?

Jim became president of the Cook County Bar Association in 1974. That same year, I became third vice president of the Cook County Bar Association. I later became president of the Cook County Bar Association in 1976.

I was Jim's third vice president. So, I was very active in all of the activities of the Cook County Bar Association. What stands out is a meeting we had with Senator [Charles] Percy, because he was considering appointing Judge George Leighton to the federal bench. That was somewhat unusual because Judge Leighton was a Democrat and Senator Percy was a Republican He did eventually appoint Judge Leighton to the U.S. District Court in 1976. We had some input into that.

Did you ever serve as co-counsel with Atty. Montgomery?

Yes, it was an enjoyable experience and it was very educational. He was excellent in assisting a young lawyer like me at that time. His method of cross-examining was excellent and I learned a lot from that.

One thing stands out in my mind when I was co-counsel with Jim. It was a murder case with four defendants. They were in a gang called the Mau Maus, charged with murder in three different counties in the state of Illinois.

What made this case so remarkable is that these were probably the most vicious men I have ever met in my life. They were all former military men. I cross-examined these men on behalf of my client and Jim cross-examined them on behalf of his client. There were four attorneys involved in this case.

What makes Montgomery different from other lawyers?

He is very thorough in case preparation. He is honest. He plays by the rules and he does not take shortcuts.

He has high integrity, good moral character. He is a friend, a mentor, and most importantly, my daughter's Uncle Jim.

POSTSCRIPT

Atty. James D. Montgomery has had a wide-ranging impact on so many of his legal colleagues. The interviews documented in this chapter were all conducted with attorneys and judges who have known and worked with Atty. Montgomery for years.

It is also notable that he has influenced other attorneys who view him as a role model and admire him for his reputation as both a highly skilled trial lawyer and generous philanthropist.

One such attorney is **Victor P. Henderson**, who—in an interview with **"Chicago Lawyer"** about his career—shared the following:

*The opportunity for me, for example, to try to be like a **Judge Pincham** or **Jim Montgomery** is inspiring. Whether I make it there or not is another issue. But, just the fact that there is so much room to grow is personally and professionally exhilarating and kind of overwhelming and daunting at the same time.*

Atty. Henderson elaborated on his admiration for Atty. Montgomery in a separate statement:

Initially, like so many others, I simply admired Mr. Montgomery as an extraordinary trial lawyer and community leader. Then, I grew to admire Mr. Montgomery as a businessman. There may be only two or three law firms in Chicago that are owned by black men, which employ more than six people, and which focus on representing plaintiffs.

Atty. Victor P. Henderson, Principal, Henderson Parks, LLC

The vast majority of plaintiffs' firms are owned by white men. Representing plaintiffs requires great skill and business acumen, because it takes a tremendous outlay of money and years of patience before such cases generate revenue—assuming they generate money at all. Part of the business risk in being a plaintiffs' lawyer is that you can lose the case after investing tens of thousands of dollars and thousands of man-hours and get no money in return.

As a lawyer for plaintiffs, you are battling huge corporations, hospitals, insurance companies, and municipalities that have no interest in paying large sums of money to the poor, powerless, and other victims of wrong-doing. Mr. Montgomery took on this challenge from a financial and business perspective and succeeded wildly. His success was even more significant for the black community because black plaintiffs' lawyers provide a unique level of empathy and respect to their clients.

Every day we live the battle of David and Goliath, personally and professionally, and we bring this experience to the arena on behalf of our clients no matter where they come from or what color they are. I don't know that I would have left the comfortable environs of my large law firm to start my own firm, but for the example set by Mr. Montgomery.

I can only hope that I am inspiring some young brother or sister the way that Mr. Montgomery inspired me. His door was always open, and I owe him a huge debt of gratitude. He mastered the law firm business game created by others and has generously shared his wealth of knowledge.

Like Atty. Montgomery, Henderson is inspired to do a great deal of pro bono work. Atty. Henderson elaborates, *"I don't think that lawyers engage in enough pro bono work. It takes a lot of courage, especially for lawyers in large law firms, where dollars count, as they should. But I think it takes a lot of courage."*

Henderson also learned early on that the practice of law is a business. A practicing CPA, having graduated from Wharton before earning his law degree at Georgetown, he believes that there is an increase in the intersection of money, business and legal issues.

He currently operates Henderson-Parks LLC, in downtown Chicago. Previously, he was the executive partner of Holland & Knight's Chicago office, supervising more than one hundred attorneys. He is also a past president of the Chicago Bar Association.

It's clear that the legacy and inspiration of James D. Montgomery, Sr. will continue for many decades to come.

Chapter 24

THE END? NOT REALLY

"Our future lies chiefly in our own hands."
Paul Robeson – Activist – Singer - Actor

Retirement has been defined as *"the act of ending your working or professional career."* Also, *"the withdrawal of a jury from the courtroom to decide their verdict."*

Capping the biography of a person who continues working is not easy. But, you've got to stop somewhere.

Now in his mid-eighties, Atty. James D. Montgomery, Sr. continues rising every day to attend to the business of James D. Montgomery and Associates in downtown Chicago.

That business includes taking depositions, making court calls and negotiating multi-million dollar settlements on behalf of clients.

And, as the media informs us each day, there is plenty of business to be had, especially in battled-seared Chicago where 2016's deaths by shooting totaled 762.

POST-COCHRAN

Once Johnny Cochran passed in 2005, Atty. Montgomery maintained his association with the Cochran Firm for several years. *"We continued to get business, but it dropped off after Johnny passed."*

A BLACK PRESIDENT COMETH!

Right about the time of Cochran's passing, a young U.S. Senator from Chicago surveyed the political landscape, concluding that it was about time that this country had its first black president.

But, not just any black president.

Equal parts Kenyan and European, **Barack Hussein Obama** was born in Kansas and raised in Hawaii and Indonesia, the son of a Kenyan father and Caucasian mother. He began his college years at Occidental College in Los Angeles, finishing undergrad at New York's Columbia University in 1983. He soon went to Chicago where he worked as a community organizer. In 1988 he was accepted into Harvard Law School, graduating in 1991. At Harvard he became the first black president of the Harvard Law Review.

Leaving Harvard he returned to Chicago becoming a civil rights attorney and professor of Constitutional Law at the University of Chicago. He then ran and won his first political office as Illinois state senator in 1996.

In 2000, the rising political novice, then thirty-nine, took on veteran **1st District Congressman Bobby Rush (D-IL)**, suffering his first and only political defeat.

In retrospect it could and has been argued that if he had beaten Rush, Obama would have never run for president, content to rise within the congressional hierarchy where only those with decades of service, get to wield any real power.

Instead, he was soundly beaten by the **former Illinois Black Panther leader**.

The postscript is, of course, history as Obama later won a seat in the U.S. Senate in 2004, becoming one of two African Americans elected from Illinois. Carol Moseley Braun was elected in 1993.

As of this writing, President Obama has completed his constitutionally-allowed eight years in office. Historians are already hard at work trying to determine what it has all meant.

I met with him shortly after he came to Chicago, Montgomery recalls. *Some of my colleagues probably told him that I was a good person to talk to when he arrived in Chicago. I would have offered him a position, but he was already working.*

The next time I encountered him was when he was getting ready to run for public office. He would come by my office and ask for my advice. I did a big fundraiser for him when he first ran for president here at the house.

President Obama and his family later became neighbors, moving to the same street as Atty. Montgomery in Chicago's Historic Kenwood neighborhood.

TRINITY UCC

Some time after arriving in Chicago, future President of the United States, Barack Obama, walked up the aisle, knelt, and committed himself to **Christ at Trinity United Church of Christ.** His spiritual mentor, **Rev. Jeremiah Wright, Jr.**, presided.

Atty. James D. Montgomery, Sr., was not just a member of Trinity, but a founder as well in 1961. In fact, Attorney Montgomery is the Attorney of Record whose signature appears on the charter of Trinity United Church of Christ. He recalls:

*"The founding of Trinity grew out of a group of people who were members of the **Park Manor Congregational Church at 70th and King Drive** (on Chicago's South Side). The assistant minister was Ken Smith. When the denomination decided that the black population was moving to the southwest part of the city, they wanted a church there. So as a member of Park Manor, I joined eighteen or nineteen others becoming the founders of Trinity."*

It has been reported that President Obama didn't just stumble into the White House. He had a plan. That included being strategic about the church that he chose to affiliate with when he first arrived in Chicago.

Trinity because of the stern, yet affectionate oversight of the scholarly Rev. Wright, was on the map as a go-to institution of worship, well before Barack Obama became a member. In a church well attended by Chicago's accomplished African American professionals…Trinity disavowed the whole concept of middle-class values. It also had a reputation of reaching out to community folk who were struggling to make it.

At one time Oprah Winfrey was a regular attendee and member. It was a place where celebrities could come and be left alone to worship. The following puts into context what Trinity is and was always intended to be, electoral politics aside.

251

Our History

We are a congregation, which is Unashamedly Black and Unapologetically Christian...Our roots in the Black religious experience and tradition are deep, lasting and permanent. We are an African people, and remain "true to our native land," the mother continent, the cradle of civilization. God has superintended our pilgrimage through the days of slavery, the days of segregation, and the long nights of racism. It is God who gives us the strength and courage to continuously address injustice as a people and as a congregation. We constantly affirm our trust in God through cultural expression of a Black worship service and ministries, which address the Black Community.

The Trinity motto:

"Unashamedly Black and Unapologetically Christian."

Of his relationship with Trinity, Obama has said, "I was able to see faith as more than just a comfort to the weary or a hedge against death, but rather as an active, palpable agent in the world."

9/11

But for **9/11**, it's quite possible that no one would have paid any attention to what church Barack Obama attended, or who he identified as his spiritual mentor.

CANDIDATE OBAMA AND REV. WRIGHT

Atty. Montgomery offers some insights:

"Clearly they were very good friends. Rev. Wright married Barack and Michelle. At some point, the Republicans realized that Jeremiah had made some allegedly outrageous statements over the years during the course of some of his sermons. Now, the press was breaking down the door at Trinity to get in. By now, Jeremiah who is very proud was starting to take offense to the criticism. Especially since Rev. Wright had retired by the time the media began its onslaught."

There was one sermon in particular that accelerated the situation: the sermon given by Rev. Wright the Sunday after the 9/11 attacks. The congregation was understandably concerned following the downing of the Twin Towers and related events on that historic day.

What's next? That was the question on the minds of many. Could it be Chicago? In a pastoral thirty-five minute sermon, Rev. Wright addressed the concerns that were on the minds of many. In that sermon, Wright calmed the fears of his congregation, giving them much-needed spiritual direction and hope.

Seven years later, when then U.S. Senator Obama announced his bid for the 2008 nomination for the presidency, the media began playing clips of the September 16th sermon, lifting out of context a particularly incendiary phrase *"God Damn America."* By doing so, the media surely provided a disservice to countless readers and listeners, many of whom believe media-invented renditions of truth and reality.

Those who hadn't heard or read the entire sermon immediately jumped to the worst conclusions, blasting Wright, Obama and the church itself for being un-American and worse.

Those who sat in the pews and the overflow room that Sunday knew that the media was wrong, dangerously wrong. What Rev. Wright had actually done was to recall a number of historical scenarios. He said in effect, that because of many past injustices to citizens, especially African Americans, it should be *"God Damn America,"* not *'God Bless America."* That's a lot different than simply saying God Damn America. Anyone who took the time to read or listen to Rev. Wright's remarks would have discovered the poetic artistry of his comments. And they served their purpose!

Atty. Montgomery says:

> At one point I attended a program in Detroit where Jeremiah was speaking on various topics and the issue came up. A few of the folks from our congregation sort of egged him on. And he went ballistic publicly blasting that whole situation and the way they had come at him.
>
> And, of course, it became extremely sensitive for Barack Obama. Now, Barack either had to embrace him or not. I remember another time when the Reverend was upset at criticism by the press. He pointed out that they had not read the whole sermon. At this point it was pretty clear that Barack had to do something. This was when he basically separated himself from him. I think that there was no question that Jeremiah was very upset about that. He responded saying, 'Maybe he will talk to me when the presidency is over,' or something to that effect.

I don't recall having any conversation with Jeremiah about what had occurred. I certainly had none with the President.

When President Obama was elected in November of 2008, Pastor Wright gave me a letter of congratulations to hand-deliver to the President. He was truly proud of him and his accomplishments.

This unforeseen occurrence set up a curious dynamic, potentially dividing the congregation against itself. Those for and against the presidential candidate. Those for and against their pastor.

Montgomery recalls:

What impact did it have on the African American community? In my opinion…I don't know that it impacted the feelings of the black community toward Barack Obama, or that it negatively impacted how they felt about Jeremiah Wright.

Continuing, he notes:

There was a lot of tolerance for anything the President did in the black community, simply because he was the first black President, and you cannot be critical of him. They came to understand that he has to make accommodations as the first black President. As far as Jeremiah was concerned, I think the deep feelings of the black community were and are behind him one hundred percent. I don't think the community believes, and I certainly don't feel, that he should in any way be criticized for those "excessive statements," which were taken out of context.

Currently, the Montgomerys attend Trinity's 7:00 a.m. service every Sunday. He has developed a good working relationship with the current pastor, Reverend Otis Moss, III, who was actually identified as Reverend Wright's replacement by Rev. Wright before all of the political controversy unfolded.

Rev. Moss was mentored by Rev. Wright for two years before being installed as the Senior Pastor of Trinity UCC. He is the son of nationally known minister, Rev. Otis Moss, Jr. of Cleveland, who is a long-time associate of Rev. Jesse L. Jackson, Sr.

Atty. Montgomery notes that, *"Rev. Moss the III is part of the healing and mentoring process with some of the younger African American protest groups demonstrating on behalf of justice and the end of police brutality in Chicago."*

Of course, this is an ongoing issue, and one that Atty. Montgomery has been involved with since he became an attorney.

When asked about his personal faith, Atty. Montgomery confides:

> *Faith means to me that I can't see God. I can't see Jesus. I don't know the details of all the biblical stories. But, I know there is a higher power in this universe because whatever is happening in this universe man can't do it, man can't hardly preserve it.*
>
> *As for me, my role in the world is to try to make the world a better place. Back in the early days when I was an idealistic young lawyer, I spent hours and days working on issues for the community. I worked on legal lawsuits challenging segregation as well as the underpayment of full-time substitute teachers who were earning less, but doing the same job as certified teachers. You know, those kinds of issues, and, then, only to find out, years later, that it's meaningless because you may change rules, but you don't change people.*
>
> *For example, Chicago was supposed to be the most segregated school system in the country in the sixties. Then, when we got the system to desegregate the schools. What happened? The whites left the school system. The Chicago Public School system is just as segregated today as it was then. So, it's like throwing the basketball in the hoop, only for it to come out again.*
>
> *My feeling then is the thing that black people need to do in order to better themselves and change their circumstances is to fight the system; the system has to be challenged frontally. And, therefore, I was very much involved in the Black Panther Party, representing them for free; very much involved in suing for Fred Hampton's murder; very much involved in just fighting the system as a defense lawyer.*
>
> *Even today, I spend sixty to seventy percent of my time performing volunteer work, whether it's on the board of a black hospital on the West Side or whether it is working to develop a thirty-acre community for Trinity United Church of Christ.*

You know, talking to students at high school graduations so they will see some role models and trying to encourage them to be committed to an education. Letting them understand that they are black, and as blacks they have obligations that go far beyond white folks.

For adults, every time I get around my "so called" middle-class friends, I am disgusted because we are sort of numb to the fact that we have all been brainwashed by the system. This is because we have been educated by the system. We think like the system. I thought like the system until I was forty years old. Ultimately, it's important for me to challenge us as well as challenge them. So, that's what faith does for me.

Full Circle, a first-hand account, is wrapped in the rich history of **Race, Law & Justice in Chicago and America** over the last fifty years. Now in his mid-eighties, with no plans to retire, Atty. Montgomery continues building his legacy, from his twenty-fourth floor suite in Chicago's financial district.

He and Pauline also spend quality time on their boat, Jim's Toy II, travel often, and laugh much. Montgomery admits that he was not a perfect father when his children were young. Nevertheless, he is proud of all his children and supports them in their professional endeavors. His children—now adults—are: Linda, James, Jr., Michelle, Lisa, Jewel and Jilian. Of his six children, three are lawyers and one is a doctor. He has five grandchildren: Gemilyn, Lindsey, Stella, Joshua, and Hannah.

EPILOGUE:

THE CHALLENGE TO THE NEXT GENERATION OF AFRICAN AMERICAN LAWYERS

The following speech was written and presented by
Atty. James D. Montgomery, Sr. to the Black Law Student Association
at the University of Illinois College of Law in 2007.

Thank you for the opportunity to share a few thoughts with members and friends of the Black Law Student Association. You represent our future, and I deem it a privilege to share with you some of my experiences over the past fifty years as a black lawyer in America.

At the outset, I want to congratulate you for having chosen The University of Illinois College of Law for your legal education. It is a great institution and accessible to those of us who have limited financial resources. I would not have been able to attend law school but for the opportunity afforded me by this great university.

I began my higher education at the University of Illinois at Navy Pier in 1949 and completed my legal education here at Illinois in 1956. My tuition ranged from $40.00 a semester in 1949 to $100.00 a semester in 1956.

Illinois has provided me with the legal education that has enabled me to compete with the best products of the Harvards and Yales of America. And, so, you will enter the profession, not as a lawyer, but as a graduate of a school that has prepared you to become a lawyer. I don't mean to in any way diminish your accomplishments in completing your legal education. What I am suggesting is that graduating is not an end in itself. It is a beginning of a process of becoming a lawyer, advocate, and member of a noble profession.

The practice of law is a drastically different pursuit from the pursuit of a legal education. It has its principles, practices, and pitfalls. Certainly, one with the ability to complete a legal education is more than capable of mastering the practice of law.

When I graduated from law school in 1956, I had no idea what the practice of law entailed. I was enamored with the careers of such great lawyers as Clarence Darrow and Thurgood Marshall — Lawyers who were pioneers in the areas of Criminal Law and Civil Rights. I had no idea of the diversity of the areas of the law practice that, at that time, were on the legal landscape.

The one principle of the practice of law that I learned early on was preparation, preparation, and preparation. That is, one must be thoroughly familiar with the legal principles and facts upon which the legal matter depends. This fact is true whether you are a transactional lawyer or a litigator.

As African American lawyers, you will be faced with a totally different and additional set of hurdles. Hopefully, the future will not be as bad as when I began the legal practice. For example, my first court appearance was in what was then a divorce proceeding. My boss and another prominent black lawyer represented one of the parties. The Caucasian judge made some racially demeaning comment that I viewed as racially insulting. These lawyers ignored the comment. It was at that moment that I determined that I would not accept any such racist treatment.

Later, when a judge said something inappropriate to me, I responded firmly, "Pardon me, your honor, did I hear you correctly?" After that, he backed down and looked at me quizzically, as if to say, "I'd better be careful with this crazy nigger." Interestingly, this is when I learned judges talk to each other. Another judge never demeaned me after that first incident.

It is critical that we challenge any effort or inclination to demean us as African American professionals. If we don't respect ourselves, we cannot expect others to respect us.

In my first year in practice, I was waiting for the clerk to call my case. An African American lawyer, who I had known and respected since I was a youngster in grammar school, appeared before the judge. He was obsequious and speaking to the judge in Ebonics-like terms. He was seeking an injunction. The Caucasian judge was condescending, paternalistic, and amused. He granted the injunction. It was one of the most embarrassing moments in my young legal career. I was stunned that this competent lawyer felt he had to behave like a clown-comic to be successful. I determined that if that was a prerequisite to success, then I wanted no part of it.

All of you are too young to have witnessed the racist radio and television drama of the 40s and 50s known as Amos 'n' Andy. One of the characters in the all-black cast was Algonquin J. Calhoun. He portrayed a stuttering, shuffling, ignorant lawyer, which was Hollywood's definition of the stereotypical incompetent black lawyer.

Fortunately, this degrading and demeaning stereotype is dead and buried. Great African American lawyers, like Charles Houston, George E. C. Hayes, Thurgood Marshall, William R. Ming, R. Eugene Pincham, as well as my

260

late partner, Johnnie L. Cochran, and many others, have dispelled the notion that somehow African American lawyers are less competent than our white counterparts.

The media, depicting of African American lawyers as somehow inferior, is not the only institution that has disadvantaged African American lawyers. Even more insidious is the attitude of potential African American clients who are still afflicted by the slave lessons of white supremacy.

My experiences in my early years—and to some extent currently—is that too many African Americans have bought into the notion of white supremacy. They believe that the white man's ice is colder than the black man's ice. This attitude is reflected in the often heard incantations, *"If you get in real trouble, you better get a white lawyer or a Jewish lawyer." "If you're real sick, you better get you a white doctor."* Or, as one of my cousins, who I don't speak to anymore, once said, *"I don't let no black person do anything for me."* Or, when I overheard my mother tell my aunt, *"I'll never hire another black lawyer."* Etc.

You've heard many more such statements that reflect the prevalence of a slave mentality, which has wittingly or unwittingly been passed on from generation to generation since the days of human bondage.

I'm sure that parents and grandparents do not deliberately indoctrinate their offspring. I'm also sure that many of them are not even aware of the impact of their communication and behavior.

Fortunately, in the sixties, there was a period when young leadership espoused black pride and led a movement to educate African Americans about the positive aspects of our culture and African Heritage. But, there is much more to be done to dispel the self-destructive disease of lack of self-love and self-esteem.

Our history did not begin in the bowels of slave ships. Our history is world history. Our African ancestors were the earliest humankind. Africans created the world's first civilizations, government systems, universities, and architectural landmarks. Africans pioneered in medicine, law, astrology, architecture, mathematics, and every field of human endeavor. Africans were the first people to sail the oceans and seas of this planet. They built the first seaworthy vessels. African Americans have every right to be proud of our heritage.

My view of Africa and Africans throughout my public education was that of an unsophisticated, simple people who grunted and bowed to two primitive white people by the names of Tarzan and Jane. What I learned in school and observed in the movies and the media was not history, but rather it was "His Story." He who tells the story decides who are characterized as heroes and who are omitted.

261

Until we, as a people, can learn our very rich heritage, and learn to love and respect who we are, we will continue to be mired in the throes of a self-defeating slave mentality. I focus on these issues because they represent the landscape upon which you will ply your trade.

There is yet another reality that you must deal with. That reality is that viable black businesses are critical to your ability to have a financially rewarding legal business. This statement is true whether you go into business for yourself or whether you work as an associate or partner in a major Caucasian law firm. The sine qua non of success in the legal business is the ability to attract paying clients. Legal talent and skills alone will not pre-ordain success.

Back in the early part of the twentieth century, there were thriving and successful black businesses. Black insurance companies, banks, and other businesses had a captive clientele. White businesses, blinded by racism, did not welcome patronage by blacks. An example of thriving black businesses was what has been referred to as the "Black Wall Street," located in Tulsa, Oklahoma in 1919 and 1920. There were hotels, banks, transit companies, grocers, insurance companies, and other successful business entities. A dollar circulated in the black business community thirty-five times before it left the community.

Today, a dollar lasts about five minutes in the black community before it goes to the white business community. The result: today, the number and quality of black businesses are diminishing. No community can thrive if all of its earnings are spent in another community.

But, these truths create for you an opportunity and responsibility. Excellence has its rewards. Mediocrity is simply not acceptable. So, I can assure you that if you pursue excellence and strive to be the best lawyer you can be, you can be successful and enjoy the rewards of a good lifestyle.

On the other hand, accepting mediocrity will doom you to failure. Not only will mediocrity assure your failure, but it will also send a message of affirmation to those who have fallen prey to white supremacy and self-hatred.

Today, there are many wonderful and varied opportunities available to young, prepared African American lawyers. When I began to practice, there were three male African American judges in the whole of Cook County, no women. There were no associates or partners in large, white law firms. There were no African American general counsels or associate counsels in major corporate law departments. There were no African American federal judges or magistrates. There were no large African American law firms. There were few African Americans in the U.S. Attorney's Office, State's Attorney's Office, or Public Defender's Office.

Today, the opportunities are boundless. You are no longer constrained, as I was, to practicing what I refer to as *"bread-and-butter law."* By this, I mean small real estate transactions, divorce cases, criminal cases, and drafting simple wills.

In all areas of practice you may choose, there are ethical and legal land mines that you must avoid. You must not be induced to violate the ethics of our great profession to make a buck.

There are clients who seek to get their lawyers to do illegal and unethical things. No amount of money can compensate you for the dishonor and humiliation of disbarment or imprisonment.

You must, by your conduct, disavow any entreaties to stray from the legal and ethical path. As you make your choices, you must understand that the law is a business as well as a noble profession.

I did not choose my cases; I took all clients who chose me. I did not calculate the time and effort required of the matter but accepted as a fee what I felt the client could afford. I did not calculate the cost of doing business and the income necessary to pay those costs and support my family. Needless to say, I had to master the art of the business of law. I hope you will be more sensitive to the business of law than I was.

A major part of my years as a lawyer was handling many public interest and civil rights matters. For the most part, this work was taxing and, largely, pro bono. I've been told that if you give Jim Montgomery a sad story, he'll represent you. Also, I was known as a good, cheap lawyer.

Many times, I would actively solicit cases and clients in high profile and difficult cases. I won my share and lost my share. I did all I could to prove (probably to myself) that I could succeed in the most difficult cases. All of this was very helpful in developing my skills as an advocate. But, it did not help me to pay my bills and support my family.

As I got older—and my children required various tuitions—I began to apply business principles to my law practice and limited my pro bono work to make money to support my family. Today, I earn millions of dollars even though I never set out to do so. I've been blessed with a good reputation both with the public, the Bench, and the Bar.

I no longer have to handle too many cases for too little money. I have a large family who survived my early penury. I urge you, nonetheless, to use some of your time and talents to better your community and those who are unpopular, despised, and powerless. It will enrich your life as it has enriched mine.

I have enjoyed all of the toys that a man or woman might want to choose. You can, too.

Ours is a great profession. Love it. Serve it well with excellence. Don't compromise your principles, and our profession will generously serve you.

Thank you very much.

AWARDS AND HONORS

Laureate, Illinois Academy of Trial Lawyers*

Honorary Fellow, Illinois Bar Foundation, 2010 - Present*

Edwin C. "Bill" Berry Civil Rights Award, Chicago Urban League, November 4, 2017

2017 Vanguard Award, Cook County Bar Association, April 6, 2017

Centennial Award: Service, Struggle, Success, Cook County Bar Association, June 21, 2014

Humanitarian Leadership Award, Millennium Builders Thurgood Marshall, November 14, 2013

Hall of Fame, Hales Franciscan High School, Donald Hubert, Esq., May 16, 2013

Trustee Award, Illinois Committee on Black Concerns in Higher Education, May 18, 2007

Scales of Justice Award, Rainbow PUSH, May 19, 2001

James A. Seaberry Outstanding Alumni Award, University of Illinois College of Law – Black Law Students Association, 2000

Hall of Fame, Cook County Bar Association, 1997

Fellow, Prestigious International Academy of Trial Lawyers, 1983

Cook County Bar Association, President, 1974-1976

*The Laureate, Illinois Academy of Trial Lawyers and Honorary Fellow, Illinois Bar Foundation are lifetime honors

ABOUT THE AUTHORS

WALTER M. PERKINS

Full Circle - Race, Law & Justice, Inside My Life, the *biography* of *nationally known Atty. James D. Montgomery, Sr., co-authored with Michelle Thompson*, is his third book. Perkins has a **B.S.** degree in Journalism from **Bradley University**; and a **J.D.** from **DePaul University's School of Law**.

Other books include: *Groove Phi Groove Social Fellowship Inc. – The First 50 Years: 1962 – 2012* (**1st Ed. 2011**); and *Write Right - Right Now – The Book* (**1st Ed. 2013**). Perkins has written for publication for more than 35 years, including magazines and trade publications. Periodicals include: *"Nation's Business," "Today's Education," "Graduating Engineer," "Dollars & Sense," "The Chicago Reporter," "N'DIGO," "The Quill," "The National Black MBA Magazine,"* and many others.

He has ghost written pieces for the *"Harvard Business Review,"* and "*Vital Speeches of the Day."* Perkins is also the founding editor of *"Operation PUSH Magazine,"* and the *"100 Magazine,"* formerly the official, national publications of the **Rainbow PUSH Coalition** and the **100 Black Men of America**. Perkins is also **Director of Editorial Services for Books Ink Literary Services**, and **Principal** and **Editorial Director, Information Plus Professional Services**.

Interviews include: **Rosa Parks, Walter Cronkite, Smokey Robinson, Professor Harold Cruse, Congressman John Lewis, Quincy Jones, Andrew Brimmer, Jerry Butler, Sir Linyard Pindling,** former prime minister of The Bahamas.

MICHELLE THOMPSON

With nearly twenty years of experience, Michelle Thompson is an independent writer, editor, and business consultant. She also serves as Associate Director of Editorial Services for Books Ink Literary Services.

Ms. Thompson, a Chicago native, began her professional writing, editing, and consulting career immediately upon graduating from the University of Illinois College of Law in 1998. She started as a writer and contributor editor at CCH, Inc., a Wolters Kluwer business and leading provider of customer-focused tax, accounting and audit information, software and services for professionals in accounting firms and corporations. Later, Ms. Thompson would serve as the Director of Operations for Francorp®, the leading international management consulting firm specializing in franchise development.